HEADLINES SOUTH WALES

★

GRAHAM SMITH

COUNTRYSIDE BOOKS
NEWBURY, BERKSHIRE

First Published 1993

COUNTRYSIDE BOOKS
3 Catherine Road
Newbury, Berkshire

ISBN 1 85306 255 3

Produced through MRM Associates Ltd., Reading
Typeset by Paragon Typesetters, Queensferry, Clwyd
Printed in England

Contents

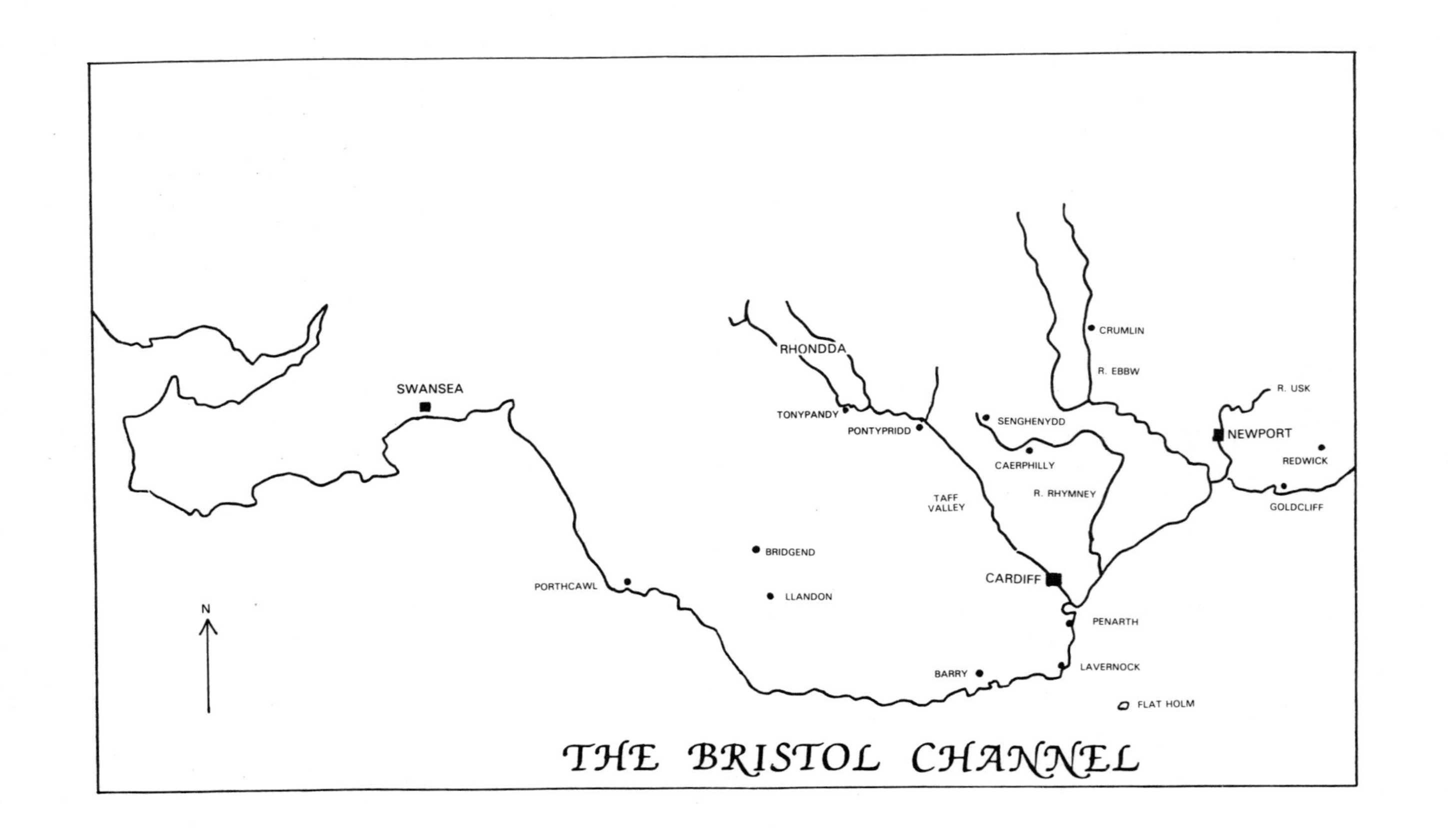
SWANSEA
RHONDDA
TONYPANDY
PONTYPRIDD
CRUMLIN
R. EBBW
R. USK
NEWPORT
REDWICK
GOLDCLIFF
SENGHENYDD
CAERPHILLY
R. RHYMNEY
TAFF
VALLEY
BRIDGEND
LLANDON
PORTHCAWL
CARDIFF
PENARTH
LAVERNOCK
BARRY
FLAT HOLM
N
THE BRISTOL CHANNEL

Introduction

★

Wales, and more especially South Wales, has been particularly fortunate in the number and quality of its newspapers – both daily and weekly. The *Cambrian* was the first weekly newspaper to be founded in Wales, being established in 1804 as a means of fostering the commercial growth of Swansea. However, it was never parochial in outlook and it faithfully reported news from all parts of the country. Twenty-five years later in the east of the country, the *Monmouthshire Merlin,* published in Newport, covered a wide area in its news gathering, and both newspapers provide a valuable insight into life in South Wales in the early 19th century.

Although the first Welsh language paper was founded in 1814 it was not until the mid century that Welsh journalism began to flourish and many Welsh newspapers managed to survive until the First World War. In 1911 there were still over one million Welsh speakers, almost half of the population. It was from this time that English mass produced papers started to make inroads into South Wales and the *Western Mail* began to emerge as the foremost daily newspaper published in Wales. It had originated in 1869 purely as a Cardiff local newspaper designed to promote the interests of the Bute estate and for many years it competed fiercely with two other Cardiff newspapers. Now the *Western Mail* is considered the national newspaper of Wales and is unrivalled in its coverage of Welsh affairs.

But perhaps the greatest strength of the press in

South Wales is found in the number of lively local newspapers still being published. Each city, town and area has its own newspaper, which though mainly concentrating on local news and affairs also cover national news. Most have a long history behind them. The *South Wales Echo* (1884), *South Wales Evening Post* (1893) and *South Wales Argus* (1892), serving Cardiff, Swansea and Newport respectively, are the best known and have the largest circulations. These and other local newspapers provide a massive archive of news and information covering the last 100 years, which gives the opportunity for fascinating reading and research.

Faced with such a rich wealth of material it is a daunting task to choose just a dozen or so stories from South Wales that 'made the headlines' and I have no doubt that some readers will question some that I have included and, perhaps more pertinently, many that I have excluded. Most of the subjects have interested me greatly over a number of years and this appeared a fine opportunity to research them in detail and bring them to a wider audience. The writing of this book has been a labour of love and I hope that my enjoyment has been transmitted to the written page.

Graham Smith
July, 1993

The By-Election that Brought Down The Government

★

In September 1922 few people reading the sad announcement of the sudden death of a little-known Member of Parliament realised the repercussions this would have on the political life of the country. The resultant by-election would lead indirectly to a serious Cabinet crisis, the fall of the Government and would bring about the demise of the ministerial career of the most charismatic politician of the time – Lloyd George.

Lewis Haslam, the Member for Newport, was returning from Burma when he was taken seriously ill and died on 18th September. Haslam was a Liberal and had represented the South Wales town since 1908. However, in the December 1918 'Khaki' General Election he had stood as a 'coupon' Liberal, in other words he was a supporter of the proposed Coalition government and because he held a 'coupon' he received the support and votes of the Newport Conservatives.

Lloyd George's Coalition 'party' was formed from Conservatives, Liberals and a handful of 'patriotic' Labour men. The election had been conducted in 'an atmosphere of national euphoria without parallel in modern times'. The Coalition was put forward as the party of national unity and led by 'the man who had won the war'. However, by 1922 the Coalition was showing serious cracks. Many Conservatives felt that the compact had long passed its useful life and some independent Liberals, led by Asquith, considered that traditional Liberal values were being lost. Together they felt that it was time to return to normal party politics. However, the threat of the Labour party, which was growing quickly in popularity, persuaded many Conservatives that their future still lay with the continuance of the Coalition.

It was in this climate of political uncertainty that the Newport by-election was held. The three candidates, in what was to prove a most critical contest, stood on the old party lines, Conservative, Liberal and Labour. As both the Conservative and Liberal candidates did not openly, nor indeed secretly, support the Coalition they

The candidates at the Newport by-election, which was fought on the old party lines after nearly four years of Coalition government. In the front row, from left to right, are Mr W Bowen (Labour), Mr R Clarry (Conservative) and Mr L Moore (Liberal). (South Wales Argus)

had to conduct their campaigns without any help from Government ministers and their supporters.

The Conservative candidate was Reginald Clarry. He was not a local man but came from Swansea, a gas engineer by profession as well as a managing director of a Swansea tin-plate works. Clarry was unequivocal in his views, 'the country is in serious need of an immediate return to sound Conservative principles in home and foreign affairs.' He stated publicly that he was proud to be 'a die-hard', as the anti-Coalition Conservatives were called, and acknowledged Lord Salisbury as his leader rather than Austen Chamberlain, the appointed leader of the party.

The Newport Liberals were in considerable disarray. Some of the local Executive wanted a Coalition candidate to stand but an influential minority demanded that an independent Liberal be selected and they even threatened to field their own candidate should a Coalition supporter be appointed. Finally a local solicitor, Lyndon Moore, was persuaded to stand as an independent Liberal. He made it clear that he supported 'the moderately progressive thought, which is found under the banner of Liberalism'. Moore had strong local connections. He was the Borough's Coroner, well respected in the town and had been an active Haslam man. One definite advantage he had was that the local newspaper, the *South Wales Argus,* was staunchly Liberal, and it nightly exhorted its readers to support him.

The Labour party fielded the same candidate that had fought the 1918 election, W.J. Bowen. He was considered a moderate and thus did not present the strong left wing policies that so frightened Conservatives and Liberals alike. Bowen was the secretary of the Postal Workers Union and since 1918 he had studiously increased his hold on the constituency and had built up a strong base of party workers and supporters. It was clear from the outset that he would be a difficult candidate to defeat. He had lost the previous election by only 3,800 votes less than Haslam and now with the votes being split three ways, he seemed the firm favourite.

It was generally accepted that the forthcoming contest would be very keenly contested and whatever the result the Coalition would certainly lose one supporter. One of the major factors in the election was thought to be the women's vote. The 1918 Reform Act had given, for the first time, the vote to all women aged over 30 years. Out of a total electorate of some 40,000 there were 17,000 women eligible to vote. Each candidate attempted to attract these votes and most commentators felt they would be crucial to the outcome.

The three candidates were formally nominated on 11th October and polling day was appointed as Tuesday 18th October. In theory this just gave less than a week for the campaign but in practice all three had been canvassing and holding meetings for the previous two weeks. At the end of September 12,000 miners were locked out of the Ebbw Vale pits and Bowen made great use of this to attack his opponents. Although 21 of the 36 Welsh MPs were Liberals, the Labour movement was making such great progress in South Wales that every seat was thought to be in danger. There was no doubt that Bowen was the front runner and at times his election seemed almost a foregone conclusion.

Clarry did not hide his opposition to the Coalition and the 'quasi-Presidential reign of Lloyd George'. However, in the main he concentrated on local issues and made much of the Government's decision, in 1921, to extend the Welsh Sunday Closing Act to Monmouthshire. Clarry opposed the decision and thus he gained the valuable support of the local licensed victuallers besides the probable votes of thousands of club members in the town. Clarry had an attractive and charming personality and seemed equally at ease facing a group of dockers as he was addressing members of the Women's Citizens Association. His wife was a great asset as she was a very able platform speaker and soon gained the women's support.

Lyndon Moore had the most difficult task, despite the strong backing of the *Argus*, which boldly asserted 'Women of Newport, Your Champion is Lyndon Moore!' He tried to unite the Liberal support in the town. Convinced that the Labour candidate was his greatest threat, he strongly attacked the 'fallacies of Socialism' in scathing terms and claimed that the Liberal party was 'the repository of peace, reform and the sanctity of the home'. Not having the 'platform presence' of Clarry or the experience of Bowen, his campaign was rather dull by comparison and his support lagged some way behind his opponents.

Bowen pursued a most vigorous and energetic campaign. He canvassed assiduously and his meetings were always well attended. Many of the big names in the party came to speak and support him – notably the Right Honourable Arthur Henderson, the leader, and a young Ernest Bevin. His confidence and that of his supporters grew apace as polling day approached. The rallying call on the last evening was, 'Victory is ours! Lloyd George must go!'

It was very apparent that the Newport voters had taken an enthusiastic interest in the election. National and local issues were fully debated and the numerous party meetings were very well supported especially considering the number of counter-attractions in the town. The D'Oyly Carte Opera Company was appearing at the Lyceum Theatre, a 'great film' *The Kid* with Jackie Coogan was at one of the cinemas, as was *Gwyneth of the Welsh Hills* with 'splendid photography'! With the by-election being covered by all the major London newspapers the town was at fever pitch during the last few days of the campaign. Perhaps the voters realised the national importance of the election for, as Clarry said on the eve of the poll, 'What Newport thinks tomorrow, Great Britain will think on Wednesday.'

When polling day dawned it was bitterly cold but thankfully dry. The booths were open from 8 am to 8 pm but by 7.30 am queues had already formed and most of the early voters were women. Throughout the day there was a very heavy turnout and a high poll was expected. The result was likely to be declared from the balcony of the town hall at 11.30 pm.

Crowds began to gather in the town centre early in the evening, even before voting had closed. Outside the town hall (now the site of British Home Stores) the road was thronged with masses of people. As an eye-witness recalled, 'The main street had a Bank Holiday night appearance. By 10 pm the crowds were dense but good order prevailed. The crowds were so well-behaved and we passed our time singing – airs from Grand Opera to "tripe and onions" and Army songs. It was a wonderful atmosphere. As the time for the declaration passed more crowded into the centre and they were now well past the Westgate Hotel. When the balcony lights of the Town Hall came on there was loud cheering and everybody became very excited. When the Mayor [Councillor E.A. Charles] with the Town Clerk [D. Treharne Morgan] appeared, along with the three candidates, it must have been nearly one o'clock. Mr

Crowds gathered excitedly in Newport's Commercial Street waiting good-naturedly for over five hours for the winning candidate to be announced.

Clarry was on the Mayor's right so we knew he had won. For well over five hours we had waited patiently for this moment. The cheering was so loud that we couldn't hear the result and when Mr Clarry stepped forward to speak the cheers were so deafening that you couldn't hear his words. Woman were waving flags, hats were thrown in the air, it was like Armistice night all over again. After about five minutes the party left the balcony but the crowds still carried on cheering and singing, it was a wonderful evening.'

Reginald Clarry had won a famous victory, He had polled 13,515 votes, with Labour second with 11,425 and the Liberals third with 8,841 – a majority of 2,090 in a poll of 80% of the electorate. Later that morning Clarry issued a statement 'The result is a great triumph for straightforward politics and a patriotic policy.' The *Daily Mail* considered it 'a decisive and historic by-election', *The Times* thought it 'an astonishing success' and the *South Wales Argus* admitted it was 'a great disappointment for the Liberal cause but nevertheless a noble victory for 'die-hard Conservatism.' The significance of the victory was seen by political analysts as 'an utter and absolute condemnation of the Coalition, a sound rebuff to Labour extremism and it paved the path to clear-cut politics, progress and reform.' But the most important factor was the effect it had on the now famous Carlton Club meeting of Conservative MPs on Wednesday 19th October.

For several months the so-called diehard Conservatives had pressed the view that the party should reject the Coalition, force an election and go to the country as a Conservative party with its own policies. A meeting was arranged by backbench Conservative MPs on the day following the Newport election and was held in the Carlton Club in St James Street, London. The meeting was addressed by Austen Chamberlain, who strongly supported the Coalition. However, another member of Lloyd George's Cabinet, Stanley Baldwin, pressed for an end to the association with the Liberals and he was eloquently supported by Bonar Law. The Newport result had an important effect on the meeting as it persuaded waverers that the Conservatives could indeed beat Labour, but only if they repudiated the Coalition. As Chamberlain tried vainly to plead with his recalcitrant colleagues, he was greeted by loud shouts of 'Newport! Newport!' The outcome of the meeting, by 187 votes to 87, was a clear mandate for the Conservatives to renounce the Coalition and to fight the election independently and strictly on its own policies.

Lloyd George leaving 10 Downing Street after his resignation. (Illustrated London News)

From then on events moved very rapidly. The Conservative members of the Cabinet resigned and Lloyd George had no alternative but to resign also and this he did at 4.15 pm on 19th October. He was destined never again to serve as a Minister of the Crown. Bonar Law was asked by the King to form a new Government although he was not formally leader of the Conservative party. The *Daily Telegraph* reported that 'the Newport result had greatly influenced the meeting' and *The Times* felt that 'the unexpected result of the by-election had strengthened the desire for independence.' Winston Churchill, another member of the Coalition Cabinet, had little say in the crisis. At the time of the meeting he was in hospital undergoing surgery for appendicitis. He later wrote 'In a twinkling of an eye, I found myself without an office, without a seat, without a party and without an appendix.'

The inevitable General Election was called, with voting taking place early in November, without time for Clarry to take his seat in Parliament. However, he repeated his victory in a two-cornered fight with Bowen and he even managed to increase his majority. The Conservatives won power with Bonar Law as Prime Minister although Churchill contemptuously dubbed Law's Cabinet as 'the Second Eleven'! Bonar Law had to resign the following May because of ill health and he was succeeded by Stanley Baldwin. Clarry became one of the founder members of the now famous '1922 Committee', which evolved directly from the Carlton Club meeting and the Newport by-election. The Committee has now achieved so much influence within the Conservative party that it is claimed that it can make or break a Tory prime minister. Its power was clearly demonstrated during the events of 1992, when the Prime Minister was forced to heed warnings from the Committee over the Government's policies on Europe and the economy. Clarry remained Newport's MP until 1929, but he was then re-elected in 1931. Four years later he was knighted and continued to serve the borough faithfully until his death in 1945. However, whatever he achieved during his political life, he was best remembered for his famous by-election victory of 1922.

Cardiff and The Spirit of Adventure

★

An annual award named 'The Spirit of Adventure' is presented by the Captain Scott Society of Cardiff to individuals or groups who in the Society's judgement exhibit the adventurous spirit as demonstrated by Captain Scott and the British Antarctic Expedition of 1910-1913. It is reasonable to question why there should still be such a flourishing society all these years after the famous but tragic expedition, and perhaps more pertinently – why in Cardiff? The short answer is that the expedition on board the *Terra Nova* left on its fateful journey from Cardiff on 15th June 1910. However, it is a bit more complex than that. Cardiff and its leading citizens played a crucial role in funding and supporting the expedition, and without the city's generous support it might never have left these shores.

Cardiff's connection with the expedition is due almost solely to Lieutenant Edward 'Teddy' Evans, who was second-in-command to Scott. Evans had been to the Antarctic with Scott and Shackleton during 1901-4 when the expedition had managed to get within 450 miles of the South Pole. The three men returned each determined to become the first man to reach the South Pole and they were all prepared to seek financial support to fund their own expeditions. As there had been very serious disagreements between Scott and Shackleton during the previous journey it was most unlikely that they would agree to co-operate, and indeed it was Shackleton who first managed to set up an expedition during 1907-1909. This time he reached within 97 miles of the Pole – a tremendous effort. At a dinner in June 1909 to celebrate his safe return Scott intimated that he would be prepared to lead another Polar expedition. However, Evans had already drawn up careful navigational plans for a swift rush to the South Pole rather than a protracted scientific project and he had taken steps to obtain financial backing for his proposal. He had written to the editor of the *Western Mail*, W.E. Davies, claiming certain family connections with Cardiff. Davies proved to be one of Evans' strongest supporters and greatly helped the cause of the proposed Polar expedition. As a result of several introductions arranged by Davies, Evans was able to convince some hard-headed Cardiff businessmen not only of his leadership qualities but also of the viability of his plans. They pledged financial aid and the use of various dock resources.

When Sir Charles Markham, a veteran Polar explorer and President of the Royal Geographical Society, realised just how far Evans was advanced in his plans, he arranged a formal meeting between Scott and Evans in the hope that they could come to a mutual agreement. At this meeting, held in July 1909, the two men agreed to combine their efforts. Evans was convinced that he could still obtain Cardiff's support for the combined expedition though Scott was rather more sceptical, feeling that 'Celtic exuberance was responsible for the assurances that Wales would do great things for the expedition.' Hitherto Scott's only connection with Cardiff had been a speaking engagement back in December 1904 shortly after his return from the Pole. Evans tried to persuade Scott that the

Lieutenant Evans' fundraising successes in Cardiff led to the decision to choose the city's port as the expedition's point of departure, and Cardiff soon became the focus of the nation's excitement. The 'Terra Nova' is seen here leaving the dock on 15th June, 1910. (Cardiff Public Libraries)

enthusiastic support of the *Western Mail*, though not yet a national newspaper, could be very important, as indeed it ultimately proved to be.

The proposed expedition was publicly announced in September 1909 and the *Western Mail* gave it very full coverage, expressing the hope that 'Wales would afford every support to the expedition'. Evans was described as 'a former Cardiff man', which rather stretched the facts. He had been born in London, his father in Lancashire and it was his grandfather who probably originated from Cardiff. The estimated cost of the expedition was put at £50,000, the majority of which would be raised by public subscription. Indeed the vessel to be used, the *Terra Nova,* would account for almost one quarter of this sum. By the end of October Evans was busy in Cardiff fund-raising, with a hectic round of lectures and private meetings. He argued cogently that the expedition would offer unlimited opportunities for advertising the commercial and civic achievements of the newly appointed city. It was during this time that Evans formed a close working and personal relationship with Daniel Radcliffe, partner in a firm of Cardiff shipowners and coal exporters, who worked energetically for the expedition with conspicuous success. By the end of December 1909 Evans was delighted to discover that £1,300 had been promised by Cardiff – over 10% of the total money then pledged. Radcliffe and Evans had also obtained free dry-docking facilities, towage and the provision of free coal bunkering. Scott was now forced to accept that he had been unduly pessimistic about Cardiff and 'Celtic enthusiasm' and when it was announced that as a result of the city's most generous contributions the *Terra Nova* would depart for the South Pole from Cardiff, the City Council and the *Western Mail* were delighted with the news.

On 1st June 1910 the *Terra Nova* left London Docks bound for Cardiff. Evans was in command and the journey was scheduled to take nine days with certain stops along the English Channel. The City Council set about making plans for the entertainment of the members of the expedition whilst the vessel was in port. However, it arrived in Cardiff Roads some 15 hours early which meant that the Lord Mayor, Alderman John Chappell, Daniel Radcliffe and Trevor Jones, the President of Cardiff Chamber of Commerce had to rush out in a tug at 8 o'clock in the evening to greet the vessel. They decided to come back the following morning for the 'official welcoming' as originally planned.

The party duly arrived at the *Terra Nova* by tug and accompanied the vessel into Roath Dock, where it tied up at noon on the 10th June. This was Scott's first visit to Cardiff for nearly six years and he was quick to thank the city officials for the generous support. However, one member of the expedition, the ill-fated Captain Oates, rather ungraciously commented 'The Mayor and his crowd came on board and I never saw such a mob – they are Labour Socialists.' Perhaps a normal reaction from a regular army officer of that time but it must be borne in mind that Oates had only secured his place on the expedition by contributing £1,000. Evans later wrote, 'We were welcomed by the citizens of the great Welsh port with enthusiasm. Free docking, free coal, defects (of the vessel) made good for nothing, an office and staff placed at our disposal, in fact everything was done with an open-handed generosity.'

Whilst in port the *Terra Nova* attracted thousands of sightseers and the officers and crew were inundated with social invitations. The highlight of the celebrations occurred on Monday evening, 13th June, when Captain Scott and his officers were entertained by over 100 Cardiff businessmen to a grand farewell dinner at the Royal Hotel, St Mary Street, whilst the crew were dined in the nearby Barry Hotel and later joined their officers. It was during the dinner that a Welsh flag and a city of Cardiff flag were formally presented to Captain Scott, who assured everybody present that they would both fly at the South Pole. By the end of the evening almost £1,000 was contributed bringing the city's total to £2,500, which was £500 more than any other city or town. The free dock facilities and fuel provided by the port were estimated at £5,000 (or well over £130,000 in current values). Of course it is this farewell dinner that is celebrated each year by the Captain Scott Society. On the following evening the expedition members were entertained to a civic reception and it was during the evening's proceedings that Captain Scott said that it was the unanimous wish of his fellow members of the expedition that the *Terra Nova* should return to Cardiff in preference to any other British port.

The following day, 15th June at about 1 o'clock the *Terra Nova* moved out of the dock with the tugs *Bantam Cock* at the stern and *Falcon* at the bow, the latter being rather appropriate considering Scott's second christian name was Falcon! A great crowd had gathered to watch the departure, all the newspaper publicity about the expedition having fired the enthusiasm of the city. There were loud cheers and in all the excitement one crew member fell overboard but he swam alongside and was quickly dragged back on board! Dr Edward Wilson, who lost his life at the Pole, recorded, 'Very enthusiastic, enormous crowds having collected at all available spots to cheer and fire guns and detonations and to make a perfectly hideous din with sirens and hooters, of which Cardiff seems to possess an infinite number.' It was a spectacular farewell and as one local newspaper reported '. . it was a scene of great emotion to watch these brave men setting forth to conquer such a terrible and frightening land. The children that were privileged to be present on this great day will be able to tell their children and grandchildren that they saw Captain Scott depart on his famous expedition.'

The *Terra Nova* was accompanied out to Penarth Pier by a fleet of small vessels as well as the two paddle steamers *Devonia* and *Ravenswood,* which were crowded with civic dignitaries and well-wishers. The *Terra Nova* was flying the Cardiff city coat of arms and the Welsh dragon at the mizzen mast, and some wag in the crew had added a leek for good measure! The Lord Mayor and other honoured guests left the vessel at the Breaksea Light, as did Captain Scott, who had to return to London on expedition business, later rejoining the vessel in Madeira. His final and prophetic words to the Lord Mayor are said to be 'I will reach the South Pole or I will never come back.'

The tragic end of the expedition and the bravery of Captain Scott, Oates, Wilson, Seaman Evans and Lieutenant Bowers have been etched into history. True to Scott's promise the *Terra Nova* with Evans in command returned to Cardiff on 14th June 1913 (almost three years to the very day that it sailed). There was a massive welcome awaiting them, with over 60,000 people at the dockside to pay their respects. Lady Scott and her young son Peter were there to greet the returning expedition. As *The Times* reported, 'Lady Scott walked the deck of the vessel inspecting the many

(Captain Scott Society)

objects of interest shown her by the officers, while little Peter wandered all over the ship. Rockets were fired and cheering came from the hundreds of schoolchildren on the banks. Commander Evans (he had been promoted in 1912) handed his white peaked cap to Peter Scott and at his behest the boy acknowledged the cheers.'

The vessel was paid off at Cardiff and it was sold back to Bowring Brothers of Liverpool. However, its figure-head was presented to the city and it now resides in the National Museum of Wales. The vessel finally foundered at sea off the coast of Greenland in 1943. There are still many reminders of Captain Scott and the expedition in Cardiff. At Roath Park a small lighthouse on the lake was erected in 1915 by public subscription. There is also a Scott Memorial Tablet in the City Hall, which was unveiled in 1916. The Alexandra Room in the Royal Hotel, where Scott and his officers were entertained, has been re-named the 'Captain Scott Room' and in the foyer are exhibits of the expedition permanently displayed. Captain Scott said 'we shall not forget our welcome in Cardiff' and in return the city has not forgotten Captain Scott and the British Antarctic Expedition of 1910.

Penarth – A Beautiful and Commodious Watering Place

★

During the last century no seaside resort with any serious pretension to popularity could hope to prosper without the provision of a pleasure pier. These unique constructions, peculiar to the British shores, were greatly beloved by Victorian and Edwardian holiday makers. The price of an admission ticket (usually 1d or 2d) bought all the delights and pleasures of being at sea with none of the attendant risks or discomforts – piers could not sink or indeed make one sick and one's feet always remained dry! A gentle and leisurely stroll along the pier to breathe in the fresh sea air, watch the maritime activities, listen to the band or other entertainment and maybe to try out the latest amusement machine; these were all indispensable and most pleasurable parts of a day out at the seaside.

It was during the 1880s that Penarth, which grew rapidly after the opening of its docks in 1865, was ripe for development. Lord Windsor, the local landowner, had ambitious plans to make the town 'a beautiful and commodious watering place – a successful competitor with other places of summer resort and one that will doubtless be very largely patronised by seaside visitors and summer excursionists.' The area was endowed with several natural advantages, including a pebble

Penarth as it was in Edwardian days.

beach, attractive cliffs and a splendid headland, from where there were unrivalled views over the Bristol Channel and across to the two Holms with the Somerset shore in the far distance. To these attractions Lord Windsor added well planned and spacious tree-lined avenues, a pleasant park, a sea wall and a fine broad esplanade, which was linked to other roads to form 'a picturesque and continuous carriage drive one mile and a half in length.' All that was missing was a pleasure pier.

The Penarth residents, and by 1891 there were 12,000 of them, were enthusiastic and quite vociferous in their demands for a pier. Many of them were successful and prosperous Cardiff businessmen who had built their elegant and substantial houses and villas in the town, making it a fast growing and rather superior suburb of nearby Cardiff. The two local newpapers of the time, the *Observer* and the *Chronicle*, strongly supported the pier campaign and frequently published editorials and correspondence on the subject.

It was in late November 1891 that 'an application for a Provisional Order for Powers to erect a Pier at Penarth . . .' was presented to the County Council. The proposed pier would be sited 262 ft from the northern end of the esplanade and would extend some 640 ft out to sea. Although the initial approval was granted early in 1892 the project seemed to lose momentum and some Penarthians expressed their concern over the delay, 'the lack of an ocean promenade will be keenly felt by those who hold the interests of our delightful town close to our hearts.' Then in the late summer of 1893 a strong rumour circulated in the town that an old pier from Douglas in the Isle of Man was to be purchased, dismantled and erected at Penarth. The editor of the *Penarth Observer* commented in September of that year '. . . any pier would be better than none. And we must ensure that another season will not be allowed to pass over without one of some sort being erected.'

The concern that the town would be saddled with 'a rusting old pier' (it ultimately went to Rhos-on-Sea in North Wales) galvanised a group of interested local businessmen to take action. They set up a company for the express purpose of building a new pier and prominent amongst them was E. Hancock Junior, a member of the Cardiff brewing family. The formation of the Penarth Promenade and Landing Pier Company in December 1893 was greeted with eagerness by local residents and the *Observer* commented 'the pier will greatly add to the attractions of our delightful town. With every Penarthian we wish it a speedy and successful fulfilment.' However, it must not be thought that these businessmen were solely moved by altruism. They firmly believed that the project was a sound financial investment. It was considered that the income generated from the pleasure steamers that would call at the landing stage at the end of the pier would ensure a handsome profit. Indeed their keen business acumen proved to be well founded as the next 25 to 30 years became the halycon days of the Bristol Channel pleasure steamers and foremost amongst them was the White Channel fleet owned and operated by P. & A. Campbell, two Scottish brothers.

The new company moved swiftly to appoint an engineer and designer of some repute in the field, H.F. Edwards, and he was also made a director of the company. His design was based on cast-iron piles to support the wooden planking or 'decking' with most attractive and finely traced ironwork railways. Compared with other contemporary piers the style was plain and formal, functional rather than ornate, however one of the features was the two shelters placed either side of the pier. They had unusual pinnacled Moghul style roofs but alas these have long since been replaced. The whole of the pier was lined with elegant gas-lamp standards. The total length was 650 ft and it was 25 ft wide, though at the landing stage it widened to 50 ft, the whole structure standing 50 ft above the water.

The contractors for the pier were James and Arthur Mayoh, two brothers from Manchester, who had immense experience in pier construction. At the time they were engaged in building Morecambe and Brighton Palace piers, had already built one at Great Yarmouth and would later complete Bexhill, the Mumbles and the Grand pier at Weston-super-Mare. The total cost of the pier has not been recorded but the Penarth Pier Company was floated on £10,000 in ordinary shares and £5,000 in debenture stock so the final expenditure must have been close to this total figure. Work started in April 1894 and by February 1895 the pier was completed ready for public use.

Saturday April 13th 1895 was selected for the formal opening of the pier and the *Penarth Chronicle* reported the scene:

> 'The Penarth pier, although having been liberally patronised for some months past as a promenade, was formally opened on Saturday in somewhat unfortunate weather. Not withstanding this fact, however, a keen interest was manifested in the event. The structure looked gay with colour, decked as it was with a profusion of flags and bunting. There were flags too, on the sea route from Cardiff to Penarth whilst the *Bonnie Doon* and the *Waverley* were both rigged up for the occasion. Shortly after 2 o'clock the former steamer left Cardiff with a goodly number of passengers. On approaching Penarth a salute was fired from the pier. It was replied to from the vessel amidst great cheers, followed by the strains of the Cogan Brass Band, whose services had been retained for the occasion. Upon reaching the pier Mr Edwards was the first to step upon the structure. There were no speeches and after discharging passengers for Penarth, the steamer proceeded for the first time this season to Weston. The operation of the *Waverley* which followed, was pretty much in the wake of the *Bonnie Doon* and the proceedings terminated . . .'

The *Bonnie Doon* was the first genuine excursion steamer in the Bristol Channel, having arrived in 1886. At the time of the opening of the pier, it was operated by the Cardiff firm of Edwards and Robertson, who were bitter rivals to P. & A. Campbell, who owned and operated the *Waverley,* which was brought into the Cardiff to Weston service in 1894.

Penarth pier became an instant success with the public and quickly became one of the most popular attractions along the South Wales coast. Special train excursions were run from Cardiff, Newport and the valleys just to visit the pier and at Penarth station there were ample horse-drawn carriages waiting to drive visitors to it. From its first summer the landing stage was used regularly by the Channel pleasure steamers and on the August Bank Holiday in 1897 no less than 30,000 people visited the pier. They could enjoy the entertainment provided by F. Darell & Co of London, which was said to be 'bright, talented, refined and just what Penarth audiences appreciate.' Penarth was one of the few piers not to have slot-machines of any description, not even the 'modern entertainments', those depiciting various 'naughty' scenes of which 'What the Butler Saw' was the favourite and most famous. They were considered 'most vulgar'' and therefore not suitable for the rather genteel character of the resort. Though Penarth with its broad esplanade, its fine parks and the clifftop walks largely appealed to the middle class and more sedate holiday maker, the pier was enjoyed by young and old alike. Near neighbour 'Barry Island had its sands but Penarth had its pier'.

In 1907 a small wooden pavilion called 'The Bijou' was erected on the sea end of the pier – prior to that time the entertainers performed in the open air! Since those long and balmy Edwardian days the pier has suffered many vicissitudes. In 1926 it was purchased by the local authority, who spent about £30,000 in repairs and restoration work as well as the erection of a concrete pavilion at the land side. This building had a cupola roof and bold dormer style windows and was

Penarth pier today; a Grade II listed building all set to survive into the next century.

originally called 'The Marina'. It was opened in May 1929 and just two days later disaster struck when most of the pier was destroyed by fire, though the pavilion survived. Restored once again the pier survived the Second World War, although of course it was closed to the public. In May 1947 it was badly damaged when a large Canadian steamer was driven broadside into it during a heavy gale. The cost of rebuilding amounted to £28,000 and it took two years to complete. The re-opening of the pier in June 1949 proved to be a grand occasion 'with sunshine breaking through as the first crowds surged on the pier.' Rather appropriately the *Glen Usk*, the most faithful and best loved of the Campbells' White Funnel fleet, came alongside with pennants flying – the pier was back in business. On the following day (a Sunday) no less than 1,000 people used the pier.

Penarth pier still stands in some of its former Victorian glory, its fine condition a tribute to the excellence of the local authority management. It is now, and rightly so, designated a Grade II listed building and still attracts thousands of visitors every year. For almost 100 years it has been an essential part of the waterfront and is held in great affection by all those who have enjoyed its amenities. It is a permanent reminder to many of those summer days of long ago when the sun always seemed to shine! As one pier-master commented, 'It was here before I was born . . . it'll be around a long time after I die!' Long may it survive.

Wales *v* All Blacks, 1905

★

There is nothing quite like an international rugby match to quicken the pulse and stir the blood of a Welshman, especially if it is being played at Cardiff. However, in December 1905 when the all-conquering All Blacks met Wales at Cardiff Arms Park, it was a match of epic proportions, such an emotional and memorable game that it has gone down in rugby history as one of the greatest internationals ever played. It was a meeting of the giants of the sport at that time, but what really made it so remarkable and famous was the disallowed try 'scored' by the All Blacks, which proved decisive to the final result. This highly charged incident has passed into the folklore of both Wales and New Zealand and has added a very special edge to all the subsequent games between the two countries. Even all these years later the mere mention of '1905' can still bring the controversy back to life.

The New Zealand touring side – called the All Blacks from their completely black strip – arrived in Britain in September 1905. They were not the first side from that country to tour, in fact in 1888 a Maori side, comprising native born New Zealanders, came and shocked the complacent British rugby world with the power and quality of their play. Therefore it was somewhat strange to find that expert opinion in this country did not expect a great deal from the 1905 tourists, but how utterly wrong these experts were proved to be. The All Blacks proceeded to win all their games with consummate

A postcard showing the gifted New Zealand rugby team of 1905.

ease, their fitness, speed, flair and technical expertise being a revelation to all. This outstanding side had developed tactics far advanced of the time and they continually staggered the crowds with the sheer brilliance of their play and the dazzling performances of individual members. Of these their captain, David Gallaher, was an outstanding tactician, Billy Wallace at full back was considered by many to be the greatest all-round player ever seen, Bob Deans, the tall and powerful centre, was called a 'Goliath of the backs' and amongst all their formidable forwards Seeling and Glasgow towered above the rest as 'commanding exponents of fearsome forward play'. So utterly convincing were their victories that the newspapers suggested that 'these Colonials born and bred were on a far higher mental and physical scale than those at home'. The living conditions in New Zealand – plentiful food, good housing, ample leisure, universal education and small healthy families – were cited as the reasons for their supremacy! And when they trounced England by five tries to nil, the question was posed 'Has the decadence of the English athlete really set in?'

The All Blacks arrived in Wales to a wonderful reception, hundreds greeting them at Cardiff station, such was the enthusiasm for rugby, which had become a major spectator sport in Wales. They came to Cardiff not only undefeated but endowed, by the popular press at least, with 'superhuman powers – they were so gifted, so versatile, so resourceful and so powerful.' The forthcoming match was likened to 'the clash of the Titans' and not without some justification, as the Welsh side was going through one of its golden eras; indeed during the period from 1900 to 1911 it won the Triple Crown no less than seven times. The Welsh team also had its own individual stars – the captain, Gwyn Nicholls, was 'the prince of three-quarters', Winfield at full back was thought to be 'the best kicker of a ball ever seen', Percy Bush on his day 'the mercurial outside half', and amongst the forwards, Dai Jones nicknamed 'Darw' or the 'Bull' and Charlie Meyrick 'a ferocious tackler', were considered the equals to any. Despite being undisputed home champions few commentators outside the Principality gave the Welsh team much chance, although a New Zealand reporter thought that 'the world's championship in rugby would be decided in Cardiff'.

Saturday 16th dawned bright and clear, which augured well for the match. From early morning the crowds converged on Cardiff from all parts of Wales and many had walked from the valleys, where rugby had become so important a part of the social life of the towns and villages. Westgate Street was thronged with supporters, vendors selling hot chestnuts, pasties, sweets and peppermints, and programme sellers – on international days this rather mundane street assumes a very special atmosphere. It was not an all-ticket match and so by 1.30 pm the gates of Cardiff Arms Park (named after the famous coaching inn that stood close by until 1882) were closed and it was estimated that over 47,000 people were in the ground waiting with increasing excitement and tension for the kick-off at 2.30 pm.

In 1948 Townsend Collins, the famous rugby correspondent of the *South Wales Argus* recalled the scene: 'Excitement was at fever heat. Never before or since have I known anything like it . . . thousands were quivering with excitement – some of us were so affected that we could hardly speak or write. The very air was charged with emotion. Hopes and fears were blended in an aching, choking anxiety . . .' The loud cheers that greeted the All Blacks as they ran out were 'a warm and appreciative Welsh welcome to this brilliant rugby side but they were nothing compared with the deafening roar that greeted the scarlet jerseys of Wales.' The Haka – the now famous Maori war cry – was heard in Wales for the first time, 'the crowd watched silently this rather chilling tribal dance.' Then followed the playing of 'Hen Wlad fy Nhadau', which had not then been fully accepted as the national anthem, indeed the programme notes suggested that the crowd might care to join in the chorus! They duly obliged with great vigour and fine voice. Gallaher later said that he had never been more impressed in his life than when he stood there and listened to the chorus resounding around the ground – 'it was awe-inspiring'. The referee was John Dallas, an ex-Scottish international who had last played for his country only two years previously. He was dressed 'in his street clothes with stout walking boots', the days of special kit for referees being still far away!

The weak sunshine, which had made the morning almost spring-like, had by kick-off time given way to a heavy mist that hung in wreaths around the ground, not quite thick enough to obliterate the game but sufficient to make the distant play rather indistinct. Wales kicked off and the long-awaited and much publicised game had started. The Welsh plan was to contain the All Blacks forwards in order to prevent them setting up their famous sweeping runs by their talented backs. This they did. Right from the first scrum they harried the All Blacks, and tackled with a ferocity that unsettled them. The Welsh full back, Winfield, kicked with precise accuracy and prodigious length and the All Blacks were not allowed to play their normal game. They had not yet met such total commitment on the tour. As Townsend Collins reported 'Men were toppled aside like ninepins, flung aside and dashed to the

The whistle and ball, (and the Welsh strip) reported to have been used in the Wales v New Zeland rugby match in 1905. (Welsh Rugby Union)

ground. It was one of the fiercest games I have ever seen. Never was there a hesitant or half-hearted tackle.' The only scoring chances fell to Wales, an attempted drop goal which just fell short and a dropped pass by a Welsh centre when he had the line at his mercy. Wales seemed in full control of the game, their much-vaunted opponents beginning to look mediocre.

The match had been in progress for about a half an hour when from a scrum the Welsh scrum half, Dickie Owen, launched an attack down the right, then suddenly switched direction and threw a long reverse pass to the left over the scrum. This change of attack completely wrong-footed the opposition. The ball was passed quickly to little Teddy Morgan on the wing, who with a subtle change of pace beat his opposing wing and after a curving 20 yards run scored a try right in the corner at the Westgate end of the ground. The crowd erupted with joy and the noise was deafening, with hats, handkerchiefs, leeks and programmes being flung into the air. One of the Welsh selectors, Arthur Gould, leapt onto the press tables shouting, 'The fastest Rugby sprinter in the world Teddy Morgan has scored!' The cheering continued for several minutes after Winfield had failed to convert.

During the halftime the crowd sang to keep up the spirits of their heroic players but in the second half the Welsh side were forced to defend with great tenacity and resilience for long periods at a time. The All Blacks continued to put greater and greater pressure on the beleaguered Welshmen, who were doggedly defending their narrow lead. Later some of the Welsh players admitted that they would have done better to concentrate on attack rather than defend their advantage. With less than ten minutes to go the All Blacks set up an attack from just inside their own half. Wallace made the decisive break and faced by the Welsh full back he passed to his left where Bob Deans was backing him up. Deans had about 30 yards to go to the line with no defender in front of him – a try seemed certain. However, he slanted his run towards the goalposts to ensure the five points but chasing him were both Teddy Morgan and Rhys Gabe, one of the Welsh centres. It was Gabe who first tackled Deans just short of the line, quickly followed by Teddy Morgan. Deans tried to ground the ball over the try line but when the referee caught up with the play he signalled for a scrum as he considered that the ball had not been grounded fairly. The crowd, who had been ominously silent, convinced that the All Blacks had scored, breathed a huge sigh of relief. Wales managed to hold on desperately until the final whistle and they had won a most memorable victory by three points to nil. Delirious supporters invaded the pitch and swarmed round their heroes, Gwyn Nicholls, the Welsh captain, being chaired off the field. The celebrations in Cardiff that night were said to have surpassed those following the relief of Mafeking! The news of the momentous victory was quickly passed to towns and villages by telephone and telegraph and some waited for hours for the returning spectators to hear at first hand the details of the amazing victory. By Sunday all 15 Welsh players were assured of rugby immortality.

The local newspapers, understandably, were effusive in their praises, 'What the other nations of these islands have failed to do has been achieved by these sons of the Ancient Britons' and 'the Prestige of Wales has been enhanced tremendously as a Nation possessed of those splendid Celtic qualities – pluck and determination.' But it was the *Daily Mail* that started the 'disallowed try' story. This newspaper which had been founded by

Alfred Harmsworth in 1896 was designed to appeal to a mass market with mainly sensational news all at the cost of ½d! The newspaper sent a telegraph to Deans, which asked the question 'Did you score?' This was despite the fact that no mention was made of the disputed try at the official dinner after the match by any of the All Blacks players. Indeed Gallaher was interviewed in the changing room shortly after the end of the match. The atmosphere between the players was said to be most friendly. The captains had even exchanged shirts and on being asked his opinion of the match, Gallaher replied 'It was a rattling good game, played out to the bitter end, with the result that the better team won; and I am content.' However, Deans' now famous reply to the *Daily Mail*, which sparked off the controversy, read: 'Grounded ball 6 inches over the line some of the Welsh players admit a try. Hunter and Glasgow can confirm was pulled back by Welshmen before referee arrived.'

The *Daily Mail* in its match report the following Monday implied that not only had Deans scored a legal try but that some of the Welsh players even admitted the fact and furthermore that Deans had been 'pulled back' from the line! In retrospect we now know that only one Welsh player held this view – Teddy Morgan – and he didn't express his misgivings publicly until almost 20 years later. Nevertheless, thus was born one of the most famous sporting controversies of all time. The furore this caused was quite amazing. Newspaper reporters at the match could not really clarify the situation as they were too far away from the spot to make a valid judgement especially considering the poor visibility. The referee felt so strongly on the matter that he wrote to the newspaper maintaining that 'Deans was tackled, he grounded the ball 6 to 12 inches short of the goal-line. At that moment he could neither pass nor play the ball, and as I passed between the Welsh goal-posts my whistle went shrill and loud . . . No try was scored by Deans.' Dixon, the New Zealand manager, and Wallace were both convinced that the ball had been grounded fairly over the line. The argument raged on and on, long after the All Blacks had left the country.

In 1924 when the All Blacks toured the country again, the controversy flared into life, fuelled this time by the ex-Welsh player, Teddy Morgan, now a doctor. During the match dinner, and after New Zealand had beaten Wales by 19 points to nil, Morgan is said to have admitted to the New Zealand captain, Cliff Porter, that in his opinion Deans had scored a 'fair try', and he even wrote his views on the dinner menu. The pros and cons of the disputed try had another full airing. However, as Deans had died in 1908, Gallaher had been killed in the First World War and New Zealand had won convincingly, it seemed an appropriate time to let the vexed subject rest.

But just six years later Wallace, in his autobiography, maintained that in 1905 the All Blacks 'had been robbed of victory'. The whole incident was once again fully debated. Then during the next tour of the All Blacks in 1935, Morgan, Gabe and Nicholls discussed the controversy in a radio broadcast. Morgan still stuck to his view that the try had been scored, perhaps the only Welshman to hold such an opinion! It was not until the 1950s when Gabe, then the Grand Old Man of Welsh Rugby, commented again on the incident, 'I confess that just for a moment, I thought Deans had made it. Then he started to try to wriggle forward. I knew the truth. He grounded short of the line. I just hung to him.' This unequivocal statement from a player so closely involved should have buried the controversy for ever, but I have no doubt that when the All Blacks next tour Wales, the incident will be resurrected by the media.

However, whatever 'the truth' of the disputed try, the 1905 match had a considerable effect on both countries. Terry McLean, the distinguished New Zealand rugby writer, considered that 'it provided a basis, a starting point, a seed of nationalism upon which all aspects of the game were to depend in succeeding years.' As far as Wales was concerned, that December afternoon demonstrated clearly that rugby football had become the national sport and that the sporting identity of 'Gallant little Wales' was firmly established.

The Tonypandy Riots

★

The mere mention of the name Winston Churchill in some quarters of South Wales will normally bring the sharp riposte 'He's the one who sent the troops in against the miners'. His part in the Tonypandy riots of 1910 earned him the undying anger and hatred of many people in South Wales. Unfortunately this legend has somewhat masked the significance of the riots but Churchill's intervention did ensure that the Rhondda, and Tonypandy in particular, became front page news.

In less than 50 years the Rhondda, really the two valleys of the Fach and the Fawr, was transformed from a tranquil and beautiful wooded valley of 'Sabbath stillness' into an industrial maelstrom of noise, waste and pollution, the river being said to be 'a dark, turgid and contaminated gutter'. Less than 2,000 people lived there in 1851 but by 1911 the figure had risen dramatically to over 152,000 – a meld of various nationalities, all crowded into the steep and narrow valleys. Indeed, it was by far and away the heaviest density of population in the country.

The conditions in the mines were hard and particularly dangerous with frequent fatal and serious accidents. The working hours were long and onerous and only barely provided a living wage. The intransigence and greed of the coal owners and the growing militancy of the miners made industrial strife common. Housing was sadly inadequate, grossly overcrowded and with poor sanitation. Infant mortality was high and diseases were rife. But despite all this, life in the valley communities was colourful and vibrant, a rich mixture of religion, music, sport and socialism fuelling a genre of literature of which the most famous example is *How Green Was My Valley*. Certainly at the time of the Tonypandy riots the Rhondda was the best known coal-producing area in the world.

Although there were many deep-seated reasons for the serious outbreak of civil disorder in 1910, the direct cause came from a long standing and bitter industrial dispute with the Cambrian Combine – a large Rhondda mining group headed by D.A. Thomas, later Viscount Rhondda. It concerned working in 'abnormal places', which arose out of the prices system of paying miners. The new seam at the Ely pit of the Naval colliery contained a lot of stone and the miners maintained, with some justification, that the price offered them to work this seam was inadequate for them to earn a permanent living wage. Thomas refused to increase 'the stone allowance' and he dismissed the 80 miners directly involved. This effectively meant a 'lock-out' of all 800 men at the Ely pit from 1st September 1910. By the following month the rest of the 12,000 miners in the Cambrian collieries came out on strike, followed a month later by all the Rhondda miners.

The unofficial strike was led by a Cambrian Combine Committee, who realised that to have any chance of success, they needed to prevent the use of blackleg labour and also close down the pumping and ventilation machinery which prevented the mines flooding. The colliery management fully expected a confrontation and indeed provoked one with their request for extra police. Over 140 members of the Glamorgan Constabulary – some mounted – were drafted into the area under the direct control of the Chief Constable,

Captain Lionel Lindsay. A similar request by the local magistrates to the Home Office for the provision of troops was refused by Churchill – then Liberal Home Secretary. This demand for military 'protection' was made before any disturbances had actually taken place!

The main body of police was concentrated at the Glamorgan colliery, Llwynpia – about ½ mile from Tonypandy's main square. It was here that the General Manager of the Cambrian Combine, Leonard Llewellyn (later described by the military as 'truculent and autocratic'), intended to make his stand and defend his 'citadel'. From early morning on Monday, 7th November crowds of striking miners gathered at Tonypandy and marched behind the town's fife band from colliery to colliery ensuring that all the pumping machinery was closed down, sometimes using force. At one colliery they stoned a new electrical power house and in retaliation were attacked by a small party of mounted police, although generally they met little opposition from the constabulary. It was not until late evening that they arrived at the Glamorgan colliery. By now their numbers had increased dramatically and they were said to be nearly 7,000 strong – men, women, youths and children – 'many waving Union Jacks and all in good humour'. It was only with the appearance of the 'arrogant' Llewellyn who taunted them that the mood of the crowd changed. The police were ordered to make a baton charge to disperse the crowd. As the *Western Mail* (a very pro coal-owner newspaper) reported, 'the apparent calm, which had distinguished the crowd in the earlier part of the evening disappeared, and after the first truncheon charge by the police upon the appearance of Mr Llewellyn there was a continued period of wild disorder.' This was in fact a gross understatement of the situation as there were many serious and brutal clashes with the police, including fierce hand-to-hand fighting, before the crowds slowly dispersed of their own volition shortly after midnight. It had been a long, cold and particularly wet day.

After this bitter confrontation, on the following morning, at precisely 10 am, the Chief Constable sent a telegram to the Home Office:

> 'All the Cambrian collieries menaced last night. The Llwynpia Colliery attacked by large crowd of strikers. Many casualties on both sides. Am expecting two companies of infantry & 200 cavalry today . . . Position grave.'

Lindsay received his reply from Churchill at 1.30 pm. It informed him that the 70 mounted and 200 foot constables of the Metropolitan Police were being sent by special train and were due to arrive at Tonypandy by late in the evening. The troops that could have been sent to the Rhondda were halted, on Churchill's express orders, at their barracks in Swindon. Later in the day he did send a message to General McCready of Southern Command that the cavalry (18th Hussars) could be moved into the 'disturbed district', effectively Cardiff, but McCready was under strict instructions not to proceed any further until specifically ordered by the War Office.

The miners were told of the impending arrival of the Metropolitan Police at five o'clock in the afternoon. Although their leaders tried to reason with them to keep the demonstration peaceful, they marched to the Glamorgan colliery where for a time the situation was relatively calm. However, when some youths started to stone the power house Llewellyn said that his men could not work under such conditions and the police were ordered to baton charge the crowds. The fighting became most fierce as one policeman later recalled, 'It was really hell. We had a terrible job driving them back... Well we could only get them as far as the Square. On that night, then, they wrecked the shops.' It was during these violent battles with the police that most of the casualties were suffered by both sides. Sadly one miner from Tonypandy later died from a fractured skull.

Most reports suggest that the fighting outside the colliery ceased about 7 o'clock and about that time a rumour went around that troops were shortly to arrive at the railway station. It was then that the anger of the crowd turned on the shops in Tonypandy. The first to be attacked was one owned by a senior magistrate, who had ordered the closure of pubs that day. In all 63 shops were smashed and looted, the only one not touched was a chemist's shop owned by Willie Llewellyn, a former Welsh international who had played in the famous 1905 match against the All Blacks. The shopkeepers later complained that there was virtually no police presence in the town (only five local constables) and that it was not the amount of goods stolen that concerned them but the 'arrogant and defiant manner' of the looters. It seemed to them to be more akin to outright class warfare and almost bordering on a revolution. One eye-witness recalled the scene, 'People were seen inside the counters handing out goods. They wore them quite without shame, almost in a festive spirit. They were not a bit ashamed... women were as bad as the men. Everything was done openly and the din was something horrible...'

The looting continued until shortly after 10 pm although by then detachments of the Metropolitan Police had arrived and most were marched directly to

Pandy Square after the riots in 1910, sparked by the rumour that troops were due to arrive. The scene had been one of 'a besieged area in wartime'. (South Wales Miners' Library)

the Glamorgan colliery. Churchill later maintained that 'the wrecking of the shops was not foreseen by anyone on the spot and would not have been prevented by the presence of soldiers at the colliery itself.'He also saw 'no reason why the policy of keeping the military out of direct contact with rioters should not be departed from.' This policy heaped opprobrium on him from the Conservative press, *The Times* thundering out 'if loss of life occurs as a result of the riots, the responsibility will lie heavily and directly with the Home Secretary.' And when it became known that Churchill had offered the strike leaders an interview with a Government industrial arbitrator (they agreed and met in Cardiff), he was told by his supporters that he hardly seems to understand that an acute crisis has arisen, which needs decisive handling. The rosewater of conciliation is all very well in its place, but its place is not in the face of a wild mob drunk with the desire of destruction.'

However, Churchill did respond positively to a further request, on 8th November, from the Chief Constable for troops to be moved into the area. On Churchill's specific orders a company of the Lancashire Fusiliers arrived at Llwynpia on the following day and the cavalry and other infantry were stationed at Pontypridd. There were further riots at Tonypandy on the 21st and 22nd of November, which were largely contained by the police and so Churchill could rightly maintain that 'it has been still possible to keep the military out of direct collision with the crowds', but on the 22nd, infantry with fixed bayonets were used on the crowd that was stoning the police. A large number of troops and police (over 1,000 strong) remained in the Rhondda until well into 1911. Indeed Keir Hardie, the Labour MP for Merthyr, likened the valley to 'a besieged area in wartime. Men, women and children have been mauled by police batons and the Press of the country have been particularly unanimous in describing the people as riotous rowdies of the hooligan type.'

Although General McCready could later claim 'Not one bullet was fired, not one sabre was raised', the presence of a strong force of troops in the Rhondda ensured that blackleg labour was used to keep the pits open, mass picketing was prevented and the subsequent trials of the strike leaders and rioters proceeded without any further outbreak of violence. The Cambrian strike dragged on until August 1911 when the miners were starved back to work on precisely the same terms as they had refused almost twelve months earlier. Churchill adamantly refused to hold a public enquiry into claims of 'police brutality' and he even congratulated the police and troops for 'maintaining law and order while a savage war was going on in the Rhondda'. The defeat of the Cambrian strike was seen in South Wales as a direct result of Churchill's intervention and his deployment of the military in the Rhondda. The Labour taunts of 'Tonypandy!' were to hound him for the rest of his political life. Even as late as 1951 he attempted to defend his policy and present 'the true story of Tonypandy to replace in the Welsh valleys the cruel lie with which they have been fed all these long years.'

The riots at Tonypandy can be seen as a manifestation of a community in crisis, where violence seemed the only way left to express their anger at the serious inequalities and injustices of a harsh and oppressive society. It took many months to clear up the effects of the night's rioting in Tonypandy but the scars left by the dispute on the people of the Rhondda took far longer to heal, as can be evinced by the bitter days of the General Strike and the Depression. As Saunders Lewis wrote in *The Deluge* in 1939:

> 'Would it not be better to stand on the corner
>   in Tonypandy
> And look up the valley and down the valley
> On the flotsam of the wreckage of men in the
>   slough of despair
> Men and tips standing, a dump of one purpose
>   with man.'

Wrecked in The River Usk

★

For those wishing to cross the Bristol Channel in the days before the Severn tunnel and the splendid road bridge there were surprisingly few problems, for even in the days of sail there were frequent ferry and market boats crossing from Newport and Cardiff to Bristol. With the advent of steam navigation the ferry services became even more regular and competition between the various vessels was quite fierce. The first regular daily steam service between Newport and Bristol commenced in October 1822 and it was advertised as 'the most economical, convenient, speedy and comfortable means of travel.' The vessels operating this service were, of course, paddle steamers, which, though greatly superior to sailing ships as far as speed and reliability were concerned, did have a tendency to roll badly in heavy weather often causing engine failure and there were certainly some rough crossings during the winter months.'

Then, in April 1844, two new iron steamers, the *Severn* and the *Avon*, both 'fitted with the new archimedean screw, high-pressure engines and built of watertight components', were introduced on the Newport to Bristol run in direct competition with the existing steam paddle ferries. These two vessels were revolutionary for their time. The first screw propelled vessel had only been trialled in 1836 and it took another five years before this technical advance was commercially developed. The two vessels had been built in Bristol and were hailed as 'two of the finest boats to leave that port' – praise indeed! The famous *Great Britain* launched in Bristol in 1843 was the first large screw vessel ever to be built and publicity heralding the new ferry service likened the two small steamers to it. They were claimed to be 'fast, comfortable and safe with elegant fittings', and even offered three classes of travel with prices varying from 2s 6d for a first class cabin to 1s for a third, as well as 'a ladies saloon with tasteful furnishings'!

However, on Saturday 4th May, just weeks after the new service had started, disaster struck. A correspondent of the *Monmouthshire Merlin,* a local newspaper founded in 1829, was strolling through St Woolos churchyard about six o'clock in the evening when suddenly he heard 'loud screams coming from the direction of the packet station'. Considering that the packet station was adjacent to Newport bridge, which is a good distance away from the churchyard perched high on the top of Stow Hill, the screams must indeed have been *very* loud. The intrepid reporter (though he probably wouldn't have recognised such a name) scented a good story and rushed to the scene. His first impressions have all the advantages of immediacy, although his style is somewhat florid and hyperbolic:

'I saw with utter dismay and disbelief the new splendid screw steamer 'Severn' amidships the river, tilting precariously so that the after part of the vessel was submerged. It was obvious that the vessel had struck the buttresses of the bridge with some force. The crowds of anxious people lining the banks of the river and the bridge were aghast with horror at the utter helplessness of the vessel caught in the vicious tidewater. It was a terrifying scene, the tumult of noise, the anguished screams, the frenzied shrieks of wild despair brought dread to one's heart. There must have been over a dozen boats frantically trying to rescue the poor unfortunate souls out of the surging and roaring waters; these brave boatmen were being urged on and cheered by the assembled multitude, which by now numbered some several hundred. The proud vessel looked in imminent danger of surrendering its life to the cruel waters of the Usk. Whole families had been drawn to this terrible disaster by the excitement and drama of this unprecedented occurrence and I will long remember those screams that came unrolling on the burdened air.'

What actually happened is described more soberly in reports that appeared in both *The Times* and *The Illustrated London News*, probably originating from the same source, our local correspondent, and I have no doubt that he would have been handsomely rewarded for the stories.

At about a quarter to six the *Severn* was berthed close to Newport bridge as the final preparations for departure were being made. It was lying with its bow facing the bridge and the stern facing down river in the direction of Bristol. There was a flood tide running and it was one of the highest of the spring, flowing at about six knots in the middle of the river and close to nine knots between the arches of the bridge. The signal was given to cast off and Ebenezer Rogers, the Captain, commenced swinging the vessel around by casting off the stern chain and depending upon the bow-rope and the power of the engine in order to bring the vessel around by its head to the tide so that it could get under way. However, there was no response from the engine and when the engineer shouted out 'The engine is blocked!', it was found that the screw would not turn. The *Severn* was now at the mercy of the fast flowing tide, which carried it swiftly towards the bridge, 'as if it was a cork', as an eye-witness recalled. The vessel's bow struck one of the stone buttresses of the bridge heavily and as it recoiled it was driven into another buttress with such a force that everybody watching on Newport bridge fully expected to see the vessel turn clean over.

It was at this point, with the vessel listing alarmingly and the decks awash with water, that most of the passengers panicked in sheer terror, certain that the vessel was about to sink under them. Edward Slaughter, one of the owners of the vessel who happened to be on board, tried to calm the passengers (of whom 20 were women) and to assure them that if they kept to the centre of the vessel they would be safe. However, about 30 decided to risk their lives to the muddy river and leapt overboard. Amongst them was said to be 'a married lady, the daughter of a highly respectable resident, with her child, followed by a matron lady and her maiden daughter and a gentleman merchant of Bristol.' There is an implied suggestion in this sentence that such respectable people should have acted more responsibly! However, all the passengers were finally saved but not without 'considerable difficulty and some delay'. The rescue was organised by Captain Richards, the Newport Harbourmaster, who fortunately was in attendance at the sailing. According to all reports the Captain showed 'great presence of mind, calm authority and commendable urgency, which saved many lives. He should be eternally thanked by those

The wreck of 'The Severn' steamer, at Newport bridge. (Illustrated London News)

fortunate survivors of this most dreadful accident.'

Meanwhile there was frantic action on board the vessel. The pumps had been rigged and manned in a desperate battle to clear the water, whilst another party of seamen was trying to save the cargo and luggage. After about an hour and a half it was quite obvious that all the efforts had been in vain and the vessel was sinking fast. Orders to abandon the ship were given. However, the Captain had left it a trifle late because as the ship's boats were launched they were immediately swamped with water and most of the crew were flung head first into the seething river. Many were carried along by the strong tide right under the bridge and some distance beyond before they were able to be rescued. Very fortunately in the whole sorry incident there was not a single life lost.

The cause of the sinking was later discovered to be a chain that had somehow firmly twisted around the screw propellor, which had caused its destruction. How the chain came to be there was a complete mystery to everybody. All the mooring chains were examined and accounted for and the Captain and crew were adamant that no spare chains had been on board. During Saturday night and all Sunday, at least during low tide, gangs of workmen tried to patch up the vessel sufficiently to enable it to refloat on the next high tide. There was a large rent in its side from the deck to the keel 'wide enough for a man to walk in and out'. Then late on Sunday evening 'a steam tug and fifteen stout brewery horses' were used in an attempt to move the vessel but to no avail. However, on the ebb tide the vessel was carried down the river for some 50 yards before it grounded again, suffering further damage to the keel and bottom plates. It was stuck in the middle of the river until the next flow tide when it was swept back to the bridge, where it settled once again in a very sorry state, with the masts snapped and most of the rigging carried away. The vessel remained there for a week or so 'on her beam-ends, a complete wreck, all hope of saving it has disappeared.' Nevertheless, the *Severn* proved to be a nine-day wonder because hundreds of people came daily from Bristol and various parts of Monmouthshire just to view the wrecked vessel – what a sad end for such a smart new little steamer. One final comment came from a Bristol newspaper, which suggested that the tragic accident had 'severely questioned the safety of screw propulsion', a rather hasty judgement on an important engineering advance especially coming from a renowned ship-building port!

Marconi and The First Wireless in Wales

★

In an age when words, pictures and documents are instantly transmitted across the world by means of satellite, it is somewhat difficult to realise that the very first faltering steps towards this sophisticated communication technology were taken such a comparatively short time ago. On a windy day in May 1897 at Lavernock Point near Penarth, a small but important piece of history took place. The successful experiment conducted on the shores of the Bristol Channel led directly and quickly to revolutionary changes in communication throughout the world.

On 11th May a young Italian, Guglielmo Marconi, made the first radio telegraph transmission across the water, 3½ miles to the island of Flat Holm. The first words sent on this historic occasion were really quite mundane – 'How are you?' A couple of days later Marconi repeated his experiment but these messages were sent right across the Channel to Brean Down near Weston-super-Mare, a distance of some 8½ miles. The age of radio communication was born.

The concept of telegraphing messages without wires was not new, even in Marconi's time, as it had been first mooted in 1838. Just 30 years later the brilliant Scottish physicist, James Clark Maxwell, had proved by mathematics rather than by practical experiment that it was indeed possible. The first practical work was

Guglielmo Marconi, in 1896 shortly after his arrival in England from Italy. (The Marconi Company Ltd.)

conducted by a German professor, Heinrich Hertz, who succeeded in producing electro-magnetic waves, which were named after him. It was these 'Hertzian waves' that fascinated Marconi.

How did this young Italian, only 23 years old, come to be at such an unlikely spot as Lavernock on the edge of the Bristol Channel making history? Part of the answer lies in the age-old saying 'A prophet is not without honour, save in his own country'. Certainly Italy's loss had become Britain's gain. That the Bristol Channel area was selected for this particular experiment owes much to Marconi's assistant from the General Post Office in London, George Kemp. Kemp was a Cardiff man and his deep knowledge of the coast was critical in the selection of the site.

Marconi was born in Bologna into a fairly wealthy Italian family. His father had retired early from a very profitable business and his mother was the fourth and youngest daughter of Andrew Jameson, the famous Irish whiskey distiller. From an early age Marconi was interested in science much to his father's annoyance, who, feeling that his son was wasting his time with such foolish experiments, wanted young Guglielmo to join the Italian navy as an officer cadet. However, Marconi's mother greatly encouraged his interest in chemistry and physics, persuading his father to allow him to attend the Leghorn Institute, and she also obtained and paid for his private tuition in electrical theory. Later she arranged for him to attend Bologna University purely to listen to lectures on physics, a rare privilege as he was not formally a student at the University. In his late teens Marconi was already conducting fairly complicated experiments on Hertz's theory of waves with equipment he had designed himself and by 1895 he had managed to send a message in morse over a distance of 2 miles at his father's large country estate. Later in the same year after improving his apparatus he decided it was time to try to interest his country's postal authority in his experiments. As he later explained 'being a loyal Italian subject I considered it my duty to inform my Government of my invention.' The Italian government prevaricated over Marconi's papers and after considerable delay they replied that they could see no practical application in his experiments.

This setback, though disappointing, did not greatly dismay nor discourage the young man or indeed his redoubtable mother. Through her Irish relatives she arranged a visit to London. Britain was thought to be the most likely country to appreciate the worth of his invention. Marconi always maintained that the primary practical application of his work was the linking of ships at sea to shore bases and after all Britain had, then, the largest maritime and naval fleets in the world.

In February 1896, Marconi accompanied by his mother arrived at Dover. His first contact with British officials was somewhat disastrous for him. The customs officers intrigued by the two large cases of equipment insisted on examining both and in the process the fragile equipment was badly damaged. Feeling that their stay might be somewhat prolonged, at least if their experience with the Italian government was to be repeated, they set up house in Bayswater and it was there that Marconi repaired his equipment and built a test laboratory. Through the good offices of his Irish cousin, Jameson Davis, Marconi was introduced to several important contacts in the electrical engineering world. In June he took out the world's first patent for a system of telegraph using Hertzian waves. Through one of his earlier contacts Marconi was invited to demonstrate his theories and experiments to William Preece (later Sir William) then Engineer-in-chief to the General Post Office and this proved to be his big break. Preece was most impressed with the young man and he had sufficient vision and foresight to appreciate the likely practical application of Marconi's work. He decided to give him every facility and offered the assistance of the General Post Office to enable him to demonstrate his apparatus and continue his experiments.

Marconi was described at this time as 'a tall, slender young man, who looks at least thirty. His dress is somewhat unusual but he has a calm, serious manner with a grave precision of speech, which further gave the idea of many more years than are his. He is completely modest, makes no claim as a scientist and simply says that he has observed the facts and invented instruments to meet them . . .'

His first experiments in England were from the roof of the General Post Office in St Martin's le Grand in London transmitting signals to other government buildings in the area. It was whilst he was working on one such experiment that a GPO worker returning from lunch looked up and shouted 'What are you doing up there?' Marconi replied, 'Come on up and I'll show you.' The employee was Kemp and from then on Kemp assisted Marconi in all his tests in this country and they became close friends for the rest of their lives.

In September 1896 on Salisbury Plain Marconi demonstrated his equipment to a large gathering of senior army and naval officers. The tests went exceedingly well and it was an impressive demonstration, but it is unlikely that any of the military men could then foresee the full potential of Marconi's invention and how it would change their world. Marconi later said of the day, 'I had the vision of communication by this means over unlimited distances. To have made such claims at that time would have been to invite the ridicule of scientists, as, indeed, was proved when five years later I had faith to believe that by the means of the system I had evolved it would be possible to send and receive signals across the Atlantic.'

Marconi was still adamant that it would be at sea that his invention would prove its worth, and for that reason he needed to test his equipment over water. Having persuaded Preece that this was the next development, Marconi and Kemp set about seeking a suitable location. They required a small island about 2 miles offshore and then, if possible, a further stretch of water across to high land for another aerial for the secondary tests. As it turned out the Bristol Channel proved to be an almost perfect situation, from Lavernock Point to Flat Holm was just beyond the prescribed distance but it offered other advantages such as plenty of space, accommodation for Kemp and his assistant and almost due south of the island on the Somerset coast was Brean Down, high enough land to suit the purposes of the experiment.

Plans and preparations started in earnest. General Post Office engineers from Cardiff erected two 112 ft masts, one at Lavernock and the other on Flat Holm, and at the tip of each mast was an aerial constructed from a zinc cylinder 6 ft long and 4 ft round. The news of the proposed experiment soon became known in the scientific world and there was a request (via the German Embassy) from a German professor, Adolphus Slaby, who was keen to attend. Slaby was also working in the field of 'wire-less communication' but was not as far advanced as Marconi. The tests were postponed for a couple of weeks to accommodate him.

On May 6th Marconi and Kemp arrived in Cardiff with all their equipment, which they stored in the GPO depot in Lower Cathedral Road. Then on the following day George Kemp and his nephew Herbert loaded everything onto a steam tug and set sail for Flat Holm. The farmer of the island, Fred Harris, helped greatly in setting up the equipment as well as providing them with a house to live in. Meanwhile Marconi had been making his preparations at Lavernock in a small field overlooking the Channel where on a fine day he could see Flat Holm in the distance. By the 11th all the interested spectators had gathered, Preece, Fardo, the Cardiff Postmaster, Gavey an electrical engineer, Williams who was head of the engineering depot at Cardiff, and Professor Slaby. If Marconi felt any nerves undertaking the tests under such close scrutiny he did

Post office engineers examining Marconi's equipment, used in experiments across the Bristol Channel in 1897. (The Marconi Company Ltd.)

not show it and he was said to be 'cool and calm in the circumstances with an aura of quiet confidence'. The signal that all was ready for the experiment was the raising of a flag and so history was made. Professor Slaby described the moment, 'It will be for me an ineffaceable recollection as five of us stood around the apparatus in a wooden shed as a shelter from the gale, with eyes and ears directed towards the instruments with an attention which was almost painful. The hoisting of the flag was the signal that all was ready. Instantaneously we heard the first tic-tac-tic-tac and saw the morse instruments print the signals which came to us silently from the island rock, whose contour was scarcely visible to the naked eye, came dancing on that unknown and mysterious agent the ether.'

All the national newspapers carried reports of the successful experiments but not in any detail nor indeed was the news given much prominence considering its importance, but after all it had to compete with the divorce of Lily Langtry (though no mention was made of the Prince of Wales) and the release of Oscar Wilde from Reading Gaol! However, *The Times* quoted Preece as saying 'the tests were very satisfactory, the invention is of assured practical value' and the local *South Wales Echo* felt that 'it would be of incalculable value to everyone involved in shipping.' Marconi was as modest as ever and he is quoted as saying, 'They are merely a batch of science notes . . . but to seafaring people they are of surpassing concern.' However, greatly encouraged by the success of the tests, Marconi decided to form, in July, a private company called 'The Wireless Telegraph & Signal Company', from which he received a cash payment of £15,000 and 60% of the 100,000 fully paid up £1 shares and his cousin Jameson Davis was appointed Chairman. One year later the name of the company was changed to 'Marconi's' but this decision was not Marconi's choice and he had to be persuaded that the change made good economic sense as his name was becoming quite well-known in the country.

In May 1898 Italy, at last, recognised the worth of Marconi's invention and its navy adopted the system – the first country to do so. At the end of the year the company obtained premises in Hall Street in Chelmsford, Essex, which became the first wireless factory in the world. The Marconi Company (now part of GEC) has always maintained a very strong presence and been a major employer in Chelmsford right up to the present day. In December 1901 Marconi achieved the first radio link across the Atlantic and six years later the first transatlantic service was set up between Nova Scotia and Ireland. Within months Marconi's apparatus was being fitted in large liners as well as naval vessels. Perhaps the most famous early example of its use was the telegram transmitted by the captain of *SS Montrose* in mid-Atlantic, which ultimately led to the arrest of Dr Crippen in Canada. Marconi became a world-wide celebrity. He won the Nobel prize for Physics in 1909 and was made an honorary Grand Commander of the Victorian Order in 1914. He spent much of his time in Italy and in his latter years he joined the Fascist party and became a close friend and supporter of Mussolini. His mother who had given him such valuable support

The small commemorative bronze plaque in the church wall at Lavernock recording a great event in the history of telecommunications.

in his early years, died in 1920 but for some reason Marconi did not even attend her funeral. There is another story there! When Marconi died in 1937 at the age of 63, he had truly become a legend in his own lifetime.

On 12th May 1947, exactly 50 years after the historic experiment in South Wales, a commemorative bronze plaque, financed by the Rotary Club of Cardiff, was unveiled in the wall of St Lawrence' church at Lavernock, close to the very field where it all started.

'Like The Crack of Doom'

★

In 1913 the South Wales coalfield was at its heyday, being the largest and most profitable in Britain. There were well over 600 mines employing almost a quarter of a million men and producing 57 million tons of coal – a total never to be exceeded. Coal was king and its wealth brought prosperity to the valleys and to the ports that exported this valuable commodity in prodigious quantities. In retrospect the year can be seen as the apogee of the amazing growth and development of South Wales, from thence the way was all downhill. However, this fabulous wealth had been wrested from the earth at a terrible human cost. The deep mines were arduous and dangerous to work, being notoriously fraught with gas and therefore very prone to explosion and fire. During the previous 75 years over 3,000 miners had lost their lives in dreadful accidents – the names of Cymmer, Risca, Ferndale, Abercarn, Llanerch, Cilfyndd and Wattstown are still remembered as tragedies on a grand scale – without the thousands of miners' lives lost due to minor incidents and the effects of coal dust. But in October 1913 the name of a small mining village, Senghenydd, would reverberate throughout the land as the scene of a mining disaster so catastrophic that it almost defied human comprehension.

Senghenydd is situated at the head of the narrow Aber valley, close to Caerphilly and about 12 miles north west of Cardiff. In 1913 the village was dominated by its two mines, the Windsor and the Universal, virtually every household in the village having at least one member working at the pits, and like so many other valley communities it was solely dependent on coal. The first shaft was sunk at the Universal in 1891 and five years later it produced its first steam coal solely for use by the Admiralty. The pit was owned by the Lewis Merthyr Collieries, a large industrial group, autocratically controlled by 'the last industrial baron' – Sir William Lewis, later Baron Merthyr of Senghenydd. The Universal had the unenviable reputation of being the most 'gassy' in the whole of the South Wales coalfield and in May 1901, just five years after its opening, the mine was shattered by a large explosion in which 81 men died. Tragic as this accident was, a far greater disaster was to hit the village.

The Universal mine had two shafts, the Lancaster, or the 'downcast', and the York, the 'upcast'. Each shaft was 650 yards deep and though coal could be brought up by both shafts it was the Lancaster that was mostly used. Underground there were three seams of coal and the workings were divided into two divisions, the east and west sides. On the west side there were six districts named after places in South Africa such as Mafeking, Pretoria, Ladysmith and Kimberley. The mine was managed by Edward Shaw, who had been there at the time of the earlier explosion. He had two under-managers, a number of overmen and a fireman for each district. The firemen were management officials responsible for safety inspections, especially to detect the presence of gas. They normally went down two hours before a shift to ensure the safety of the workings. The total number of men and boys employed underground was 950, of which 440 worked in the west side.

On Tuesday morning, 14th October, just after six

The Senghenydd pit ablaze on 14th October 1913; thousands flocked to the scene, some in anguish for their relatives trapped in the mine, some drawn by morbid curiosity to this dreadful disaster. (Photo: Cardiff Public Libraries)

o'clock 935 men and boys descended the Lancaster shaft for the day's shift, which was due to start at eight o'clock; it took an hour or more for the men to walk to their coal face workings. At ten minutes past eight there was a terrific explosion, which shook the foundations of the village and the sound of the blast was said to have been heard in Risca in Gwent almost 10 miles away as the crow flies. One of the survivors later described the tremendous explosion as 'like the crack of doom'. Such was the awesome power of the blast that it roared up the Lancaster shaft forcing the cage before it and thrusting it into the winding gear above ground, in the process smashing the wooden platform into a mass of splintered pieces. Among the debris was found the first victim of the disaster, the banksman (in charge of the pit shaft and winding operations) whose body had been decapitated by a large wooden splinter. Dense clouds of smoke and dust poured out of the shaft and it was only when this slowly cleared that the full force of the explosion could be seen in the twisted wreckage of the carriage.

As the *Daily Mail* reported, 'The shock which announced the explosion sent a tremor of anguish through every dwelling . . . Men and women rushed to the pit in their hundreds, dreading to learn the worst and with them, for school had not begun, hurried pale-faced, frightened, and crying children. Most of them, without food all day, were still keeping their painful vigil well into the night.' Within a minute or so of the explosion half of the Universal mine was ablaze. Soon a message was passed around the waiting crowds that contact had been made with those trapped underground and some of their fear and anxiety was allayed but then nobody was aware of the true enormity of the disaster.

The manager, along with some volunteer night shift miners, began a descent by the York shaft. Less than 150 ft down the smoke and fumes were almost unbearable but they continued downwards until they reached the first seam. Their way was blocked by tangled girders and the heat was intense. However, by using a long and painful detour, they managed to make their way to the Lancaster shaft where 'a very heavy fire was raging' – as one of the party said 'it was like looking into a furnace'. News reached them that the men in the eastern section of the mine were safe and it was now clear that it was in the western section that the explosion had occurred. The manager considered that there was little hope for those miners trapped behind the wall of fire. He was now faced with several serious problems. There was no water supply as the pipes had been destroyed in the explosion, the timber props were burning furiously and collapsing causing additional roof falls, and because the Lancaster shaft was a downshaft air was being drawn in to feed the flames and circulate the heat and deadly fumes. Shaw was only too aware that to reverse the ventilation system would take several hours, valuable time that he could ill-afford, so he decided against this course of action, a decision which would be strongly criticised at the official enquiry. With no breathing apparatus and no adequate means to fight the fire the small party of rescuers were forced to return to the surface and seek help.

As the news of the disaster quickly spread, rescue teams from the neighbouring valleys arrived on the scene. It was far into Tuesday night before the rescuers managed to break through the barrier of fire. They worked tirelessly and bravely in extreme and dangerous conditions. It was said that when they returned to the surface their clothes were smouldering and they were physically exhausted by the intense heat below ground – indeed one of the rescue party was killed by a roof fall. By dawn on Wednesday it was estimated that 428 men were still trapped. Despite the intense heat, the raging fires, roof falls and the presence of heavy gas the rescue parties worked ceaselessly but any realistic hope for the trapped miners was fast disappearing. On Thursday an official report was made stating that 512 men had been rescued alive (5 later died in hospital), 53 dead bodies had been recovered but 364 were still missing and the statement ended chillingly 'all hope is abandoned of finding further survivors.'

It was now all too clear that Senghenydd had become the worst mining disaster ever. Messages of deep sympathy flooded in from all over the country. The new King, George V, gave £500 to the disaster fund, which had been organised by the Lord Mayor of Cardiff. All the national newspapers carried poignant pictures of the scenes around the pit-head, images which even now still convey the sheer horror and abject sorrow of those families caught up in such a ghastly disaster. It is sad to relate that thousands of people flocked to the village drawn by some macabre and morbid curiosity just to be present at the scene. They came by train, carriage, car and on foot and by Sunday it was thought that nearly 250,000 people were crowded in and around Senghenydd, the road from Caerphilly being said to be blocked solid.

The rescue work continued unabated though it would have needed a miracle to find any survivors. The fire was not finally controlled until the following Monday and still the search continued for weeks upon weeks. More and more bodies were recovered and many were so badly disfigured that they could only be identified by their possessions, which were laid on top of their shrouded bodies. The final death toll was 439 (including 33 bodies still unlocated in the mine). Of this appalling total more than 60 were less than 20 years old and eight were only 14 years. Each household in the village was affected by the tragedy. One widow lost her three sons, the youngest being only 14 years old. In one house there were no less than eight deaths – a husband, four sons, two brothers and one brother-in-law. Senghenydd was left with 205 widows, 542 fatherless children and 62 aged parents without financial support. Three years later the village rugby side contained 13 players under the age of 16 because there were so few older players left. Each dependent family was given about £300 from an official fund and a further 10s per week from the public subscription fund, a meagre recompense for the loss of a breadwinner, even in those days when the average weekly wage of a miner was £2 11s.

The corner of Penyrheol cemetery where many of the victims of the Senghenydd explosion are buried.

The official enquiry opened in the Law Courts at Cardiff on 2nd January, 1914, and continued until 21st February. Despite over 20,000 questions being asked, no conclusive answer was reached as to why or how the explosion had occurred. Two theories were put forward as likely reasons. One suggested that a fall of coal freed a pocket of gas which was ignited by the shorting of the bell wires. Another opinion, which many miners subscribed to, was that the explosion came from the naked flame kept in the lamp room some 440 yards from the bottom of the pit, which ignited gas released from a roof fall. Following the enquiry, Shaw and the Colliery Company were charged with minor breaches of safety regulations and after several appeals they were found guilty on eight counts and fined a total of £24! The

South Wales Miners Federation utterly condemned the court's finding and they were supported by public opinion – one newspaper headlined 'Miners lives at 1s 1¼d each!'

As Jan Morris has commented, 'Senghenydd 1913 presented to the world the saddest image of Wales'. But life in the village had to continue and the Universal mine was still worked until its closure in March 1928. The most permanent reminder of the tragedy is to be found on a number of gravestones in Penyrheol cemetery, most of which bear the simple but sad epitaph 'Died in the Senghenydd Explosion'.

Barry – The Finest Dock in The World

★

When the steamship *Arno,* dressed overall in flags and pennants, proudly entered the new Barry Dock on 18th July 1889, its arrival brought to a fitting and splendid climax one of the most ambitious engineering projects ever undertaken in South Wales. The opening of the dock realised the hopes and faith of a group of far-sighted industrialists and entrepreneurs, and more especially it fully justified the vision and enterprise of one man, David Davies of Llandinam, because without his vigour, drive and determination the dock would not have been built.

Davies was the epitome of the self-made Victorian man. Born of poor parents, he received little formal schooling, but as a young man had made a success of both farming and timbering (hence his nickname 'Top Sawyer'). Then he turned his talents to bridge building and railway engineering, gaining considerable eminence in Wales. In his middle age Davies became a prosperous coal owner, entered politics as a Liberal MP and later was knighted by Queen Victoria. This varied and very successful life made him a multi-millionaire and he was probably the most famous Welshman of his day, considered a giant by his contemporaries. Despite all his famed successes, the pinnacle of his life's work was the development of Barry Dock and it is for this achievement that he is remembered today.

The statue of David Davies overlooking his dock at Barry.

The origins of this quite amazing project can be traced back to 1864, the year in which David Davies was persuaded to purchase a coal lease in the upper Rhondda valley at Treorchy. Coal was mined at his Maerdy pit in 1866 and within eleven years Davies had five mines working in the area, collectively called the 'Ocean' Collieries', producing almost one million tons of coal a year. The phenomenal growth of the South Wales coalfield had caused considerable problems for the railway and dock companies. Because of severe congestion coal wagons were taking up to 15 or more hours from the Rhondda to Cardiff docks when the journey should have taken only a couple of hours. Once the coal arrived at the Bute docks the berths were so full that two to three hundred vessels were often seen at anchor awaiting a place. In 1873 David Davies warned the Taff Valley Railway Co to provide a better service but the situation did not improve, in fact it deteriorated as the amazing growth of the Rhondda pits continued. Despite continuing and costly delays, it was one single action by the Bute estate that proved to be the catalyst in persuading Davies and his fellow coal owners to take some positive action. In 1882 Parliament agreed to a proposal from Lord Bute to build another new dock at Cardiff and to increase the shipping charges. Although they were never levied, the threat of them was sufficient for Davies and his fellow owners to seek an alternative solution. They were now determined to provide further dock accommodation along with a better rail link and they were quite prepared to undertake such a large project at their own expense, confident that they could make the new dock pay.

At a meeting in the Ocean Collieries' office at Cardiff docks in June 1882 it was decided to find an engineer of repute to prepare plans for the new dock and the railway from the Rhondda. The civil engineer selected for this task was John Wolfe Barry, son of Sir Charles Barry, who had redesigned the Houses of Parliament. John Barry, as well as having a very appropriate name for the project, had been involved in many railway projects including the London underground. Henry Mark Brunel, son of the famous Isambard Kingdom, was appointed as Barry's assistant and together they formed a formidable and experienced team.

The site selected for such an ambitious project was

Barry. This small and isolated country village was some 7 miles west of Cardiff with a population of less that 100 living in thatched cottages, with just one shop, the old thatched Ship Inn, a ruined castle and a small but ancient tidal harbour. Just off the mainland was a small island, which only 80 years earlier had been a notorious smugglers' haven. When later asked why Barry had been chosen, one of the promoters said 'We were desirous of having a dock as near as possible (to the Rhondda), but in a position in which we would not take any of Lord Bute's land.' Actually there were more positive reasons for selecting Barry. It was situated further down the Bristol Channel so vessels could enter an hour earlier and leave an hour later than at Cardiff. There was also a great depth of water at low tide, and furthermore as Barry offered protection from storms it had long been used as a shipping haven. But perhaps the most telling advantage of the site was that the local landowners, Lords Windsor and Romilly, were active supporters and investors in the scheme.

The Barry Dock and Railways Bill was presented to Parliament in April 1883 and a battle royal commenced. The Bute estate fronted a furious opposition in defence of its vested interests and the Bill was ultimately rejected by the House of Lords after over one month's bitter and acrimonious debate. Undaunted by this set-back Davies and his associates re-presented the Bill the following year. This time, after further long debate, it was passed and received Royal Assent on 14th August 1884. It had certainly been the stormiest passage of any Bill for many a long year. Much of the ultimate success must be given to David Davies, who greatly impressed the Select Committees with his evidence and convincing arguments. When questioned on whether he could find sufficient money to fund the project, he said he would be very pleased to send the money up in coal trucks in gold sovereigns if they wanted sight of it! With the passing of the Bill one prominent Welshman is reported as saying 'This is the greatest event that has happened in connection with our country for over half a century.'

The new company – Barry Dock and Railways – was authorised to raise £1,050,000 in £10 shares (at this time a miner earned about 15s a week) and to borrow £350,000 to finance the project. Lord Windsor was appointed Chairman and David Davies contented himself with the post of Deputy Chairman but he was always in full command of the massive operation. Some of the biggest names in the South Wales coal and shipping industries were directors and they lost no time in selecting and appointing a highly reputable contractor, Thomas Walker, who had also been contractor for Preston docks as well as the Severn Tunnel.

The construction work started in November 1884 amidst great ceremony. A contemporary report says that 'A select group of dignitaries and industrialists, most dressed in top hats and frock coats, solemnly assembled on Castleland Point [close to the present dock authority building] where Lord Windsor cut the first sod.' On the following day the *Barry and District News* commented that 'It was a symbol of great things to come in these ancient parishes of Barry, Cadoxton and Merthyr Dyfan. Soon the green fields will begin to disappear as the new and important seaport of Barry grows apace. A time of unimaginable change lies ahead. As well as the tens of thousands of people who are confidently expected to settle in Barry, vital facilities will have to be provided – hospitals, schools, shops and offices . . . The mind reels at the magnitude of the challenge that confronts us.' A note of caution was then introduced, 'Do not be afraid of change, so long as it is not change for its own sake, and so long as what is good and fine in our inheritance is not carelessly put aside.' Certainly no place in South Wales would grow as quickly as Barry. It was said that when the first explosion was fired in November, the blast killed an owl and a rabbit, which was evidence of 'the isolation and quietude of the area'.

Soon Thomas Walker's navvies appeared in great numbers and it was said that at the height of the construction over 3,000 were employed night and day, 'great lusty figures, rough in manner, terrible figures and hard as nails . . .' A visitor to the excavations in February 1887 described the scene, 'Clouds of steam emitted from something like a score of locomotives, which were continually passing to and fro, as well as from a number of steam excavators, cranes and grabs, completely enshrouded the operations. The only cheerful prospect appeared to be the new stone houses, which studded the hill sides of what is known as Walker's Town or East Barry.' The massive engineering project – the dock was planned to be the largest in the country at 73 acres in extent – was also described as 'entering Dante's Inferno – the noise, the steam and the bustle defies description.' Over three and a half million cubic yards of earth had to be removed and no less than 200,000 cubic yards of masonry built. During the whole construction work there were 150 fatal casualties and over 500 serious injuries and these appalling statistics were considered 'normal for such a project'!

The construction of the dam to exclude the tidal waters from an area of 200 acres caused considerable problems mainly because of the high tidal range of the Bristol Channel. The eastern dam was completed in July

1885 and the western side just nine months later. An entrance channel with two breakwaters leading to a basin, which served as an antechamber to the dock itself had to be constructed. The 27½ miles of railway from Barry to Pontypridd was completed late in 1888 and the first train ran on the line on the 22nd November. By June 1889 the dock was ready for the water to be let in. Early on the morning of the 29th June Wolfe Barry inspected the gates, which were the first in the country to be operated by hydraulics, and at 9.30 am his daughter operated the lever which opened the gates to the basin. About 15 minutes later the main entrance to the docks was formally opened by a wife of one of the directors. It must have been an impressive sight to see this great extent of dock being filled by the waters of the Bristol Channel. There were still minor works to be completed on the dock and the official opening was planned for three weeks hence.

Thursday 18th July 1889 proved to be a hot sunny day but with a light cooling breeze from off the sea. The day was observed as a public holiday in both Barry and Cadoxton so a large crowd was expected for the official opening. The pier-head and the area around the basin were decked with flags, streamers and bunting. Outside the dock, near the breakwaters, there was a myriad of small craft all flying flags and bunting adding to the 'carnival atmosphere of this great occasion'. Two special trains were run from Cardiff to bring the directors and their families, as well as the 2,000 distinguished guests.

The trains arrived punctually at 10.15 am and David Davies conducted Mrs Lewis Davis, the widow of one of the earliest and strongest supporters of the project, to the extreme edge of the quay where the red, white and blue sik ribbon lay across the entrance to the dock and with just a few words Mrs Davis took up the large dagger-shaped knife of 'Damascus steel' and cut the ribbon. As it was seen to flutter free, there were loud cheers from the crowds of people lining the quays – over 10,000 was the estimate – the workmen blew steam whistles and guns were fired. The *Arno* from Sunderland towed by the tug *Levant* and steered by T.R. Thompson, one of the directors, proceeded slowly into the dock. This vessel was followed by a yacht and a long string of tugs and pilot boats. At the rear came several cargo vessels and by 11.30 am the first truck of coal was tipped in the *Ravenshoe*. Barry Dock was in business!

There was a slight hiatus at the official lunch. It would appear that the waiters went on strike demanding that their wages be doubled. David Davies was intransigent. He refused their claim and when the guests appeared

The SS 'Arno' entering Barry Dock, 18th July 1889. (Photo: Welsh Industrial and Maritime Museum)

he explained the position and asked them to help themselves. When the waiters saw what was happening they returned to work, but in his speech Davies specifically asked the guests not to leave any tips! At one stage during the proceedings Thomas Walker, the contractor, could not be found. He was at the other end of the dock where he had arranged a special lunch for all his workers and navvies. He seemed to be enjoying their company far more. As it was pointed out this was the measure of the man. 'He cared for his workers. He built houses for them and their families as well as a hospital and a school . . . He was far in advance of his time as an employer, one who really cared for his employees.' The festivities continued for a fortnight and medals were distributed to all the children in the area as well as to those members of the committee who had organised the opening ceremonies.

Barry Dock became a roaring financial success almost overnight. David Davies addressing shareholders in September 1889 said 'The dock, as you know, is fast filling with ships. We have the finest dock in the world . . . We have finished a work which might be called gigantic; we have done it well and cheaply.' It cost in fact £2 million, close to £70 million in today's values. A second dock was opened in 1898 and by 1901 Barry's coal exports exceeded those of Cardiff. By 1913 over 11 million tons of coal were exported, making it the largest coal exporting port in the world. Not everybody was quite so happy with the vast changes and the local Liberal MP said in 1892 '[Barry] is a large rapidly growing town, intent on nothing but money making.' One result of the building of the dock was that Barry Island was no longer an island, but was joined to the mainland by a causeway and over the next 30 years it developed into a most popular seaside resort.

Unfortunately David Davies died in July 1890 after a long illness, not living long enough to see the full potential of his dock realised. John Barry collaborated on the building of the Tower Bridge in 1894 and was knighted in 1897. Thomas Walker went on to construct the Manchester Ship Canal. The steamship *Arno* sank in February 1899 off Portsmouth with a full cargo of coal. Sadly Barry Dock is now a mere shadow of its former glory, with coal shipments ceasing in 1976. However, the statue of David Davies, unveiled in 1889, stands proudly overlooking the dock and town of Barry which he created, and is a reminder of the days when the port was the world centre of the coal trade.

Escape from The Welsh Colditz

★

Most people are familiar, through such films and books as *The Wooden Horse, The Great Escape* and *Colditz,* of the many valiant escape attempts by Allied forces from German prisoner-of-war camps during the Second World War. However, what is less well known is the large and audacious escape by German prisoners from a camp in South Wales. This bold and well-organised attempt took place in the latter days of the war in Europe and proved to be the biggest of its kind in Britain. For about five days the exciting story of the chase and capture of the fugitives made the headlines of all the national newspapers despite the restrictions of wartime censorship.

The prisoner-of-war camp was situated on the main A48 road just about a mile south of Bridgend. This ancient market town came into prominence when coal began to be mined in the valleys to the north. During the Second World War a Royal Ordnance Factory was established on the edge of the town, which attracted labour from the surrounding countryside and neighbouring valleys. It was this large munitions factory that led indirectly to the prisoner-of-war camp. Because many of the workers, predominantly women, had long distances to travel, it was decided to build hostel accommodation nearby at a place called Island Farm. However, the project proved to be somewhat of a white

Island Farm, Camp 128, as it is today; in 1944 it was chosen as a suitable site for captured German Officers.

elephant as most of the women opted to travel rather than live in the drab and cheerless huts. The site remained empty until 1943 when some of the large influx of American troops into the country were based at the camp, where they remained until after D-Day (June 1944).

During the early months of the campaign in France large numbers of German troops were captured and places had to be found in Britain to hold them captive. The Island Farm site was thought suitable for captured German officers, indeed the accommodation was considered 'too comfortable for other ranks'! The first inmates arrived amidst great secrecy late one November evening in 1944. As they detrained at Bridgend station they appeared far removed from the popular belief of cowed and dispirited prisoners. They were swaggering and arrogant and as they marched along the Merthyr Mawr road to the camp they sang *Deutschlund uber Alles* and other patriotic songs; indeed many were fanatical Nazis and amongst their number was a fair sprinkling of SS officers.

The Commandant of the camp, now numbered '198', was Lieutenant-Colonel Dorling, a World War I veteran, who had been a prisoner-of-war in Germany and had made a successful escape. The camp was not completely ready for the prisoners as the huts had to be converted, barbed wire fences and watch towers needed to be erected as well as arc lights installed. It was certainly ill prepared for the some 1,600 prisoners it was planned to contain. Some of the work on the perimeter fences was completed by the prisoners under the close supervision of the guards but this enabled a few of them to gain valuable knowledge of the barricades as well as the area surrounding the camp.

In retrospect it can be seen that escape plans were made very soon after the first prisoners arrived. In January a tunnel was discovered during a surprise search by guards, sited under a concrete block in one of the huts. The Commandant was convinced that this was a 'decoy tunnel' deliberately sacrificed to allay suspicion and induce a complacent and relaxed attitude amongst the guards. He felt that 'We must be more alert than ever. I am quite certain that there is another tunnel being dug somewhere else in the camp, because tunnels are never dug singly.' However, there seemed to be no increase in the security measures or checks as a result of the discovery.

Then on the night of Saturday 10th March 1945, the Commandant's words of warning were proved to be all too correct. At 10 o'clock in the evening the first prisoners escaped by means of a tunnel dug from hut 9 to a spot just outside the perimeter wire. The escape was meticulously planned, a strict timetable being enforced in order that each group of three men knew exactly when to arrive at the hut. The prisoners' drama group put on a specially loud performance to mask any unusual noises from the huts. By 2.15am no less than 66

A view from inside one of the camp huts, where prisoners plotted and planned their escape via tunnels that would be ventilated, reinforced and equipped with electric light!

prisoners had used the tunnel without the guards' knowledge. As the next prisoner left, he was spotted just outside the perimeter fence and challenged by one of the guards and, as he did not stop, he was shot in the shoulder. The alarm was raised and the guards immediately searched the fence and one of them actually fell into the tunnel opening, much to the delight of the watching prisoners. Eleven prisoners were quickly captured in the vicinity of the camp and the Commandant ordered an immediate head count and for some unaccountable reason the numbers were found to be all correct. The local police superintendent, who had immediately been informed of the break-out, commented 'It could have been a lot worse if there really had been a mass escape'. At that time 55 German prisoners were at large in South Wales.

When the tunnel was closely examined by the guards, it was found to be most professionally constructed. An 18-inch square of thick concrete floor had been removed from one corner of the hut and the tunnel went down some 18 ft and was almost 60 ft long, finally coming up in a ploughed field just outside the fence. It was equipped with a ventilation system and electric lights powered from the mains supply. It was later disclosed that the guards had received a prior warning about movements outside the huts but had not taken them very seriously, and it was not until the duty officer arrived back from Bridgend Conservative Club that he ordered a search in the area but no hut was entered by the guards. The prisoner that had been shot had acutally 'gate-crashed' the escape – he had not been briefed on the correct procedure and furthermore he was carrying a white kit bag which had been spotted by one of the guards.

It was not until roll-call the following morning that

the true enormity of the escape was discovered. A full alert was called and road blocks were set up covering a 15 mile radius from the camp. But by this time many of the groups had got clean away. As the prisoners were recaptured they were found to be well equipped. All had maps of southern Britain and the French and Irish coasts but as the routes showed railway lines rather than roads they were thought to have been traced from maps in railway compartments, again evidence of the very early preparation of the escape plan. Many had small compasses made from magnetised razor blades and all the prisoners were well provided with food, toasted bread, butter, corned beef, marmalade and plenty of cigarettes, and this only seemed to justify the locals' firm belief that the prisoners were receiving more and better rations than they. Actually the food store at the camp had been raided shortly before the escape. The escapees left in groups of three, the leader being a member of the SS, the second man a navigator, pilot or seaman and the third member an English speaker. It was never discovered who had master-minded such a well-planned and meticulous escape but it was thought that well over 600 prisoners had been involved in the plan.

Such a large escape could not be kept quiet by the authorities and although the local newspapers were silent on the matter, the national papers took great delight in reporting the escape in full, causing acute embarrassment to the camp guards, the police and the military. Headlines such as 'Planes hunt 55 men in Welsh valleys', 'Vast Game of Hide and Seek led by thousands of armed troops goes on' and 'SS men in Mass Jail Tunnel Escape' abounded. The antipathy of the locals to the prisoners was very real. The rumours of better food and the so called 'comforts of the camp' rankled and the loud martial songs and deliberate howling that came from the camp were found to be most disquieting. Many people were disturbed by the arrogant attitude of the prisoners as they marched to and from work details. Indeed the police were concerned for the safety of the escaped prisones should they be captured by the locals.

Some of the escapees did not get very far. The first two were picked up by a local police constable at Llanharan, just 8 miles from Bridgend. They were lost! On Monday, five were found hiding in a copse at Laleston, again not very far from the camp. Eleven were recaptured as they were walking along a country lane. There was some police concern when it was thought that a woman in Porthcawl had been shot by some of the escaped prioners when she refused them money and food. This rumour incensed those who were hunting the escapees. In the end it transpired that her Canadian 'husband' – he was an Army deserter and had a wife in Canada – had shot her. Before she died she incriminated him and he was later tried and executed.

One enterprising group stole the local doctor's car and managed to get as far as the Forest of Dean before it broke down and their hiding place in the forest was discovered by farm workers. They made their escape and for two days wandered about the countryside until they jumped a goods train, which was loaded with ammunition. The train stopped at Castle Bromwich near Birmingham airfield and one of the group, a Luftwaffe pilot, spent two hours reconnoitering the airfield with the intention of stealing a plane. They planned to lie low during the day and return the following night. However, they were cornered by farm workers armed with shotguns before they could put their audacious plan into operation. Another two managed to get as far as Eastleigh near Southampton by train before they were picked up in a railway yard thoroughly exhausted. These two had covered the furthest distance of all the escapees – 180 miles. A week after the escape the last three were captured by an ex-policeman after a two mile chase near Glais in the Swansea valley. They said that they were glad it was all over but thought it had been 'good sport'!

On their return to the camp none of the escaped prisoners were punished, though some claimed that they suffered brutality at the hands of the guards. By the end of March all the prisoners at the camp – over 1,600 – were moved to 'unknown destinations'. The full inquiry into the escape brought strong criticism of the security procedures at the camp. Many recommendations were made for improvements, all eminently sensible and one would have thought that they should have been in operation right from the inception of the camp. However, Island Farm was now prepared for a more important function. It was re-designated 'Special Camp 11' with plans to receive 160 German officers holding the rank of General, Admiral or Field Marshal.

The arrival of these high ranking German officers at Bridgend caused quite a stir. It seems that when they arrived at the station they were met only by a police superintendent and a small Army escort. These haughty prisoners adamantly refused to carry their luggage, they demanded transport to the camp and furthermore they expected to be greeted by a high ranking British officer. This protocol difficulty was solved quite simply by Mr Hill, the stationmaster. He put on his resplendent GWR stationmaster's uniform and peaked cap, which was covered in rich gold braid and facings, and appeared in front of the generals. They assumed from the splendour of the uniform that he must be a most senior officer and they meekly obeyed his order to pick up their luggage and march!

For the next three years Special Camp 11 held captive some of the highest ranking officers of the Germany army and navy. Field Marshals Von Rundstedt, Von Kliest, Van Manstein and Von Brauchitsch spent much time there. Several of the prisoners were ultimately tried and convicted of war crimes. Many were still ardent Nazi supporters but the most hated man at the camp was Major-General Dornberger, who was the V2 rocket builder. In 1947 he was taken to America to work on space rockets. Admiral Voss was another inmate. He had been responsible for the U boat campaign in the Atlantic and he acted as the camp liaison officer. A person who lived close to the camp later said 'The prisoners' presence was felt due to the terrible singing – they sang a great deal at night and this kept me awake.' The camp was finally closed in May 1948. Since then the site (some 22 acres) has been deserted and allowed to fall into disrepair. The huts and other buildings, although still standing, are dilapidated, doors and windows are smashed and everything is now overgrown with weeds and brambles, although the outline of the camp can still be traced from the concrete roads. One of the huts has become a listed building because of the murals and paintings on the walls executed by the prisoners. In 1992 there was a plan to develop the site as a 'unique visitor attraction' but this did not materialise. The site now belongs to the Mid Glamorgan County Council.

The Noble Viaduct at Crumlin

★

It seems a great shame that the thousands of visitors bound for the Garden Festival at Ebbw Vale in 1992, should have missed a view of the famous Crumlin viaduct, but alas it was dismantled and demolished 26 years earlier. This 'Noble Viaduct', as one Victorian writer described it, was in its day a railway and civil engineering marvel, which attracted tourists from far and wide. A *Guide to Wales* published in 1885 described the area, 'the valley of the Ebbw is famous for its remarkable viaduct, which spans the valley with a spider like lightness . . . it is hemmed in by lofty hills, thickly clothed with trees and shrubs on either side. The hills touched by the extremities of the viaduct cast their shadows upon the river, and in the summer months when the river and the canal, which run parallel, glisten in the sunshine, the neighbourhood of the viaduct presents scenes of unsurpassed natural beauty quite equal to the lakes of Westmorland.' This picture of silvan loveliness has somewhat changed, a century of industrial development having taken its toll, but in all fairness the valley is now slowly recovering its past splendour and beauty.

Prior to the coming of the railway Crumlin was a quiet hamlet on the banks of the river Ebbw some 12 miles north of Newport. There were a few miners' cottages, a 'company' shop and the Navigation inn on the side of the canal. But, in 1851, the decision of the Newport, Abergavenny and Hereford Railway Company to extend its line to Merthyr and Dowlais to the west changed all that. The Taff Vale extension, as it became known, made sound financial sense, offering an increase in iron and coal traffic from the Taff valley to the industrial Midlands. However, in engineering terms it was likely to prove a colossal and daunting enterprise with the need for cuttings, embankments, bridges, tunnels and the ultimate challenge of crossing a deep valley gorge at Crumlin.

With typical Victorian boldness and confidence the project was embarked upon. A competition for the design of the viaduct was offered. The cost of building a stone bridge some 200 ft high was quite staggering and therefore several engineers submitted plans for an iron construction but it was the design by Thomas Kennard of a lightweight iron bridge that won the day and the contract was duly awarded to Kennard & Sons of Blaenafon in 1853. Kennard's design was revolutionary in concept and its advantages were the relative ease of construction with a far shorter building time and much greater economy as compared with a conventional masonry structure. Kennard planned to use open crossbraced iron pillars to support the structure and, as the heaviest piece of ironwork would weigh less than one ton, it could be lifted up by a small crane and a series of pulleys. The type of construction – the first of its kind – would also allow for expansion and contraction due to temperature changes; furthermore the iron girders were designed to deflect by ⅝ inch when a fully loaded train passed over them and then to return to their original form once the train had passed.

Kennard started upon the construction work without delay. He established a local works for the receipt of the wrought-iron bars from his Blaenafon works, which would then be fabricated on site, thus, of course, further reducing the costs of the project. Iron tubes and castings came from the company's other works at Falkirk in Scotland, first by sea to Newport and thence by either rail or canal to Crumlin.

The total length of the viaduct was 1500 ft from hill to hill and it would be supported by eight piers, each connected by iron girders 150 ft long. From the railway line to the bottom of the valley was just under 200 ft or slightly below the height of the London Monument. At the time of the construction only two other viaducts in the world would exceed it in height and length. It also proved to be the most economical structure of its kind ever built, the total cost being a mere £62,000. This figure contrasted most vividly with the Britannia Bridge over the Menai Straits, which was stone-built and although 20 ft longer was of the same height but had cost almost ten times more.

Less than seven months after the construction work had commenced, an official ceremony was arranged for the foundation of the first pier situated in the central part of the valley. On 8th December 1854 Lady Fitzmaurice, wife of one of the directors, and a goodly number of spectators watched while the very first girder was raised very slowly by steam winch at a rate of four inches a minute. It was reported that when the first girder was 'planted' to connect the two piers, 'loud and hearty cheers burst from the lips of the workmen, some of them in most perilous positions, while one, more courageous than the rest, actually walked across the girder, which was about a foot wide and two hundred feet from the ground.' Indeed it seems that amidst all the excitement Henry Kennard, the brother of the constructor, climbed upon a platform and spoke to the men 'in glowing terms of the dangers to which our troops were exposed in the Crimea, proposing to them the desirability of contributing something towards the fund.' He must have been quite persuasive as his proposal was received with 'deafening exclamations' and every man offered a day's pay to the fund – a gang of 20 men was paid in total £5 per day. After a bottle of wine (not champagne!) was broken over the pier and a cup containing current coins was placed in a recess of the brickwork, the column was formally named the 'Isabella pier' after Lady Fitzmaurice. The guests then departed for the inevitable official lunch, which seemed to be an integral part of such functions, whilst the workmen were entertained 'to a measure of refreshments' in the permanent workshop, which had been built close to the viaduct.

The viaduct took three and a half years to build and unlike many other Victorian construction projects, it was almost accident free with just one fatality – a remarkable safety record. In the process Kennard also developed Crumlin village, building workers' homes, places of worship, a reading room, some shops as well as a hotel. The last of the girders was lifted in place on 17th December 1855 and the construction of the railway was started by Liddell and Gordon, the engineers for the line. The double railway track was laid on very stout timber some 26 ft long. By May 1857 the whole structure was ready for a severe testing. On the 8th, in the presence of Professor Gordon and Mr Carr of Liddell and Gordon, the Kennard brothers and scores of railway and construction engineers, one engine was run onto the viaduct, followed by another until there were six engines and one waggon weighing no less than 380 tons just supported by one span of ironwork of 150 ft in length. This stringent test was far in excess

The great Crumlin viaduct. (Illustrated London News)

of the weight expected under normal working conditions. Indeed Mr Carr with 'a nerve that startled all present, got over the rails of the bridge, and clinging to the iron-work alone minutely examined the works to discover if there was any giving way of the parts so strong was his conviction of the safety of the structure'. Several days later the government inspector examined and tested the bridge before he expressed his unqualified admiration both for 'the elegance of the work and its stability'.

After passing the safety tests with such flying colours the railway company decided to open the line to public transport on Whit Monday, the first day of June. Intense preparations for the big day were planned. Excursion trains were arranged to run from various parts of England and Wales, and these were to be gaily decorated with flags, ribbons and flower garlands. According to the local newspapers, on the day 'the whole of the Ebbw valley assumed an air of festivity and a general holiday spirit' but the focus of the celebrations was Crumlin itself. The railway station was festooned with bunting, flags and flowers and the centre of the viaduct was spanned by 'an arch of evergreens and flowers from which hang banners inscribed ''Long Life and Prosperity to T.W. Kennard'' and ''Long Life to the firm of Kennard Brothers''. Two strings of flowers stretched from the base to the summit of the bridge.' Cannons were placed on both sides of the valley and these were fired at regular intervals during the day, the sound reverberating through the valley and as an eye-witness recalled 'they rolled around the air like extraordinary loud claps of thunder.'

It was estimated that over 20,000 people were present for the opening and when the first train rumbled over the viaduct, there were 'loud shouts and cheers accompanied by the roar of the cannons and the music from the band, it made it a most spirit-stirring occasion.' Whilst the important guests, some 150 in number, adjourned to Thomas Kennard's newly built and palatial house, appropriately named Crumlin Hall, to attend the official dinner, the rest of the spectators enjoyed various attractions – funfairs, fortune booths and side-shows of many descriptions. They were even allowed to walk along the viaduct but were warned to beware of the trains, although a speed limit of 8 mph had been imposed! Indeed this speed restriction remained in force for the whole working life of the viaduct. A special medal was struck for the occasion with a picture of the viaduct on one side, and the particulars respecting the structure on the reverse. It was said that the medals sold 'in large quantities', however, not many have seemed to have survived.

At the dinner there were many speakers, all eulogistic

to the talents and skills of Thomas Kennard and they all agreed that the viaduct was one of the finest in the world and 'a triumph of engineering construction'. As a result of the success of the Crumlin viaduct Kennard obtained contracts to build bridges in Spain, Italy and India as well as the Tees Bridge. The traffic using the viaduct quickly developed and continued to increase annually. In 1866 there was a slight concern to find that the timbers were showing signs of wear and the floor of the viaduct was replaced with wrought-iron girders, which did not then require renewal until 1925. In the late 1950s about £10,000 was spent on repairs. Other than repainting (15 tons of paint) every five years or so, these were the only maintenance costs of this remarkable structure in its century of use. The viaduct was retired in 1964, though it was still fully serviceable and two years later it was completely dismantled and demolished. However, before it was taken down it received some fleeting fame featuring in a film called *Arabesque* starring Gregory Peck and Sophia Loren.

Had the viaduct managed to survive another 20 or so years I am sure that in a more enlightened age it would have been permanently preserved as a splendid and elegant example of Victorian enterprise and engineering skill. As it is, Crumlin viaduct only remains in the memories of those people, including the writer, who were fortunate to see this 'enormous harp of the winds.'

The Triple Crown Air Disaster

★

On a peaceful Sunday afternoon in the delightful countryside of the Vale of Glamorgan there was an appalling air disaster, which brought grief and tragedy to virtually every valley and town in South Wales. The aircraft, which was on charter, was returning from Dublin and had on board 78 passengers, all of whom had flown over to support the Welsh rugby team playing Ireland at Belfast. The crew of five and 75 of the passengers perished in the crash, making it then the worst air accident in aviation history. The sheer enormity of the disaster touched everybody in Wales and as a Belfast newspaper aptly wrote 'There is a shadow across the sun in Wales, the singing in the valleys has abruptly ceased.'

The fateful year was 1950. In January there were positive signs of a resurgence of the Welsh Rugby XV, which for many years had languished in the doldrums. The team had gone to Twickenham to play England and had won a very close game, their first victory there for 17 years. Well over 20,000 faithful and devoted followers had travelled to support the side, many of whom failed to see the match because the gates were closed some time before the kick off. It was after this match that it was decided to make future internationals at Twickenham all-ticket affairs. The supporters for Wales were so numerous and the singing so strong that

South Wales Argus

LIGHTING-UP 6.42 p.m. to 6.01 a.m. — IN 58th YEAR OF PUBLICATION — THE SIZE OF THIS PAPER IS DICTATED BY THE GOVERNMENT

REGISTERED AT THE GENERAL POST OFFICE AS A NEWSPAPER — NEWPORT, MONDAY, MARCH 13, 1950 — THREE HALFPENCE

THIRTY-FOUR OF THE AIR CRASH VICTIMS WERE FROM MONMOUTHSHIRE

Doctor, Magistrate, Rugby Players and Officials Are Among the Dead

Disaster Unparalleled in Recent Times in Wales, Says Coroner

On the Spot Descriptions by "South Wales Argus" Reporters

The worst tragedy in civil aviation history near Cardiff on Sunday struck a cruel blow at Monmouthshire.

About half of the eighty people killed when the Tudor V. airliner crashed at Sigginston, near Llandow Airport, its destination, on Sunday, were from the County, – some of them well known in Rugby football circles.

THE WESTERN VALLEY SUFFERED MOST.

SEVERAL OF ABERCARN RUGBY CLUB'S PLAYERS ARE DEAD.

ABERTILLERY, ABERCARN, RISCA, LLANTARNAM, GARNDIFFAITH, BLAENAVON—THESE ARE BUT A FEW OF MONMOUTHSHIRE'S TOWNS AND VILLAGES OF MOURNING TO-DAY.

SONS AND HUSBANDS—SEVEN WOMEN WERE AMONG THE VICTIMS—HAVE BEEN LOST.

The Tudor aircraft, biggest aeroplane ever to operate from Wales, crashed on its return from the Wales-Ireland Rugby international in Belfast.

Only three survived the crash.

Two of them were from Llanelly. They were the last to board the plane at Dublin on Sunday. They escaped with cuts and bruises; the other survivor is in hospital, and is stated to be progressing favourably.

OPENING THE INQUEST AT LLANDOW ON SEVENTEEN VICTIMS, THE CORONER (COLONEL HAROLD REES) SAID: "SUCH A CATASTROPHE AS THIS HAS BROUGHT ANGUISH INTO HUNDREDS OF HOMES IN SOUTH WALES AND ELSEWHERE, AND HAS BROUGHT SORROW INTO THE HEARTS OF ALL THE PEOPLE OF THIS COUNTRY.

"The disaster is unparalleled in recent times in South Wales, and it is comparable only to the great colliery disasters of the past.

"In times of war one is expectant and ready perhaps to meet disasters of this kind. Many of those who died in this crash had survived the War.

"Our sense of grief must be made greater because at the time of the accident all these people were returning to their homes after having been on a festive occasion."

The two Llanelly men, Gwynne Anthony, of 1, Neville Street, Llanelly, and his friend, Handel Rogers, 26, Gower View, Llanelly, who were travelling in the tail of the aircraft, walked away from the twisted, mangled metal of the ill-fated airliner.

They crawled to safety through the crumpled fuselage, and escaped through the broken back of the sky giant.

One of the men, suffering from shock, was looking for his shoe, lost in the crash, when found by rescuers.

Thus, while the triumphant Welsh team were led by a band through the Cardiff streets, lined with cheering and joyful people, eighty of their supporters who had cheered them to victory less than 24 hours before lay dead.

Listed in the casualty lists were people from all walks of life—miners who had saved for the treat of a life-time, business men on a football holiday, a doctor, a Justice of the Peace.

Not one Monmouthshire passenger survived the disaster.

Of the total of 83 people in the plane, 73 were killed instantaneously when the impact occurred. Ten were extricated alive, but of these, all except three died later.

Don Rowlands, the Abercarn Rugby captain, his right centre, Douglas Barnett picked to play for the National Coal Board trials on April 5, Ray Bos, the Abercarn coach, and ex-Welch Regiment soldier, Jack Robins, who followed Abercarn team wherever they played, were included in the long list of fatalities.

Two other Abercarn men, Mr. Mark Lewis, 45, and Mr. Bert Watkins were among the men early known to be dead.

A Monmouthshire J.P., Mr. Perry Thomas Jerman, 53, a master builder in Risca, who made a habit of seeing as many international Rugby matches as he could and whose brothers' names will be remembered as Newport Rugby players in the early thirties, died in the crash.

With him in the Risca party were also Dr. Alec Paterson, of St. Mary Street, Risca, Mr. Peter Blunt, 37, married, with three children, Mr. Reg Beavis, haulage contractor, Mr. Austin Morrisey, "mine host" at the Railway Tavern—not one survived.

Mr. Perry Jerman, J.P.

Day of Sorrow

Sunday was to be one of the happiest days for Mrs. Jerman, Mother of two boys she was celebrating her 25th birthday when news of the crash and with it the news of her J.P. son, became known.

Convoys of ambulances, drawn from all parts of Glamorgan, were rushed to the scene of the disaster, which surpasses in its gigantic death roll even many major pit accidents.

The first ambulances were at the scene just 15 minutes after the nose of the airliner had buried itself into the heart of a green field.

As the last ambulances arrived at the R.A.F. hospitals at Llandow and nearby St. Athan grim-faced and apprehensive relatives of the victims were arriving and asking for news of their kin.

There were many sad faces and many brave people in the waiting room of the hospitals. Many did not need to be told the news. As they entered the room the face of a young corporal told them of the fate of their loved ones.

A 21-year-old girl who died in the crash was Miss Barbara Patricia Thomas, who lived with her parents at the Lamb and Flag Hotel, Glyn Neath, where she helped her parents. She accompanied Mr. Daniel Nelson, 70, who owned an electrician's business at Glyn Neath, and his brother, Mr. Morgan Nelson, 60, a tobacconist from Glyn Neath. Both were killed.

One aged man, the proud father of an only son, heard the news of the crash on the wireless. He was driven from Port Talbot, but his son, veteran major of the Burma battle, was dead.

"I Saw It"

An eye-witness account of the crash was given to a South Wales Argus reporter by a number of young men who were kicking a football in their back yard at the time the plane crashed.

They were the first to reach the air liner.

Thomas John Newman, 27, who lives in Cardiff, was visiting his parents' home at the Cottage, Sigginston.

He said: "The time was almost twenty past three when we heard the plane flying very low. We could see that it was only about thirty feet above the ground. It looked as if it was trying to avoid the house.

"Then the engine stalled, and the plane nose-dived into the ground.

"We left our game and rushed about 100 yards to where the plane had crashed. Nothing could be heard when we got there.

(Continued on Back Page)

South Wales Argus
Editor ... ... Tel. 2245
News Editor ... ... Tel. 2246
Reporters ... ... Tel. 4001
Commercial and Advts. . 2244
Telegrams: Argus, Newport.
London, 150, Fleet-st. 3336 Cen
Monday, March 13, 1950

Sympathy and Sorrow

TRAGEDY comes to South Wales and Monmouthshire, — tragedy out of the air, in the worst accident in the history of civil flying. The tragedy seems the more terrible since it involves the deaths of so many supporters of Welsh Rugby football, returning from a scene of national triumph. What can be said after a disaster which has brought so much grievous loss to our valleys? In the stricken homes, sympathy to-day will seem small consolation in the face of death brought with such stark suddenness, but we offer it sincerely and heartfelt. That is a sentiment in which we know the general public will join. But while we sorrow—as the whole civilised world will sorrow—with the friends and relatives of the victims of the crash, it is inevitable that there arises in the mind recognition of the far-reaching issues involved. It is essential that no effort is spared at the Inquiry to ascertain the exact cause of the disaster, and that no relevant fact shall be hidden from the public. In that way, terrible though this accident is, it may in time make some contribution towards further minimising the risks of air travel. A disaster with such a heavy death roll must necessarily give rise to questions of a searching character, but we should endeavour, through our tears, to view this incident against the background of the millions of miles of accident-free air transport flown annually. Each day air travel is becoming safer; to-day we know the sky is the highway of the future, and that British air lines, backed by native ingenuity, can lead the world. So it is vital that the Llandow air crash should not become an instrument of uneasy reaction against flying. This is a tragic hour in which to plead for a practical attitude, but it must be done in the interests of justice to air transport, and it in no way lessens our genuine feelings of sympathy and sorrow towards those who have suffered so much in the calamity which has befallen them.

No Decision on Petrol for Holidays

DUKE LEAVES CAIRO

This photograph shows the Tudor V., broken in two where it crashed in the field about 300 yards from the air-field at Llandow.

Vice-marshal Saves Reporter

MINISTER SAYS—

Our Hearts Go Out to Welsh People

PUBLIC INQUIRY IS PROMISED

The Welsh airliner crash was mentioned in the House of Commons on Monday.

Mr. Beswick, Parliamentary Secretary, Ministry of Civil Aviation, replying to Mr. Churchill's question as to whether there was any statement on the air crash, said: "The Minister (Lord Pakenham) asks me to say that he cannot adequately express his regret at this tragic happening of yesterday. Our hearts go out to Wales and the Welsh people in their hour of sorrow."

Ireland's Distress

A Brave Woman

An Ace of Spades was on the Floor of the Inn Bar...

ON THE FLOOR OF THE BAR AT THE 18th CENTURY INN GREENHOUSE, LLANTARNAM, WHEN IT WAS OPENED ON MONDAY MORNING WAS A PLAYING CARD.

It was the ace of spades—superstitiously regarded as a card of ill-omen: of death . . .

From the Greenhouse last Friday, seven friends set out in a shooting brake for Cardiff to fly to Ireland for the Ireland v. Wales Rugby international.

Only one came back—Mr. John Maggs, of Llantarnam, who changed his Tudor flight ticket for a Dakota flight to Ireland . . .

The other six, including the licensee of the inn, Mr. Bert Butcher, were killed in the crash on Sunday.

In the inn on Monday it was business as usual.

Mrs. M. Butcher, wife of the licensee (he would have been 62 in May), decided to carry on, because "it would have been his wish."

Squadron-leader W. H. Irving, D.F.C. (Cwmbran)

Married Twice

Mr. Herbert Butcher

THE CASUALTY LIST

A full list of names and addresses of the seventy-seven victims who have been officially identified appears on Page Three.

Mr. W. J. Stevens (Cwmbran)

CERCOPSIS CHICKS

In the field 300 yards from Llandow airfield lies the wreckage of the Tudor V. aircraft, in which eighty lost their lives returning from the Rugby international match in Ireland. Two Llanelly men walked out of this tangled mass from their seats in the tail.

(Courtesy of South Wales Argus)

an English reporter said that unless they were careful Twickenham would end up as 'one of the more famous Welsh grounds'!

The second match of the championship took place at Swansea in front of a capacity crowd and Scotland were beaten very convincingly. Now even the most pessimistic supporter began to feel that this might just be Wales' year! Therefore the game against Ireland in Belfast planned for March 11th would be decisive. Though Ireland had lost very narrowly against England, they had trounced Scotland and it was freely acknowledged that they had a very strong side so it was likely to be a very hard-fought game especially as the Welsh team had a chance of winning against all three – that coveted result known as The Triple Crown. Given the wonderful support the Welsh team had received at Twickenham, it was not surprising that some 8,000 devoted fans were expected to travel to Ireland to cheer their team to victory.

The fateful charter flight was arranged by Mr Harry Dunscombe of Cardiff, who had originally planned two flights but later decided two trips were rather ambitious as he was not sure that he could sell all the seats. This was in the days when commercial flying was still in its infancy and charter flights were something of a novelty, especially to follow a football team. The cost of the fare was £10 5s, no small sum in those days and probably equivalent to £150 in today's values, and most of the passengers had saved for many weeks for the weekend trip. At first the number travelling was restricted to 72 but in the last week before the flight another six were added and the cabin was adapted to accommodate them.

The aircraft, a Tudor V, was chartered from Fairlight Limited of Langley in Buckinghamshire, whose Managing Director was Air Vice-Marshal Bennett, a well-known RAF pilot from the Second World War. The company had two Tudor aircraft, both of which had spent much time recently operating on the Berlin airlift. The Tudor aircraft, manufactured by A.V. Roe & Co Ltd, had a somewhat chequered design history and there had been several accidents with earlier marks in which the likely causes had not been clearly established.

The aircraft, G-AKBY with call-sign 'Star Girl', arrived at RAF Llandow on Friday 10th March. It was commanded by Captain A.J. Parsons, a very experienced pilot with over 3,000 flying hours and of these 300 hours were in command of Tudors. The flight to Llandow went without a hitch and it arrived safely, in fact it was the largest aircraft to have landed in Wales. The airfield was an operational RAF base that was not geared to commercial flights, for instance there were no facilities to weigh baggage, a point that was discussed at some length at the subsequent accident enquiry.

There were no problems on the outward flight and the plane landed at Collinstown Aerodrome at Dublin. For the passengers there was plenty of time for shopping, sightseeing and perhaps a little drink before travelling on to the big match. As expected it turned out to be a very exciting game. It was closely contested from the start and at half time there was no score. A couple of minutes into the second half Wales scored a try, which was unconverted, only for Ireland to equalise with a penalty goal. With only three minutes remaining Wales scored their second unconverted try in the corner. The last minutes were tense but the Welsh team held on grimly and the game was won by six points to three. The Triple Crown had come back to Wales after

39 years. The headlines the following day were ecstatic: 'The Triple Crown is ours! Cymru am Byth!', 'Forwards Magnificent' and 'Wales' Greatest Hour'. That Sunday morning all Wales savoured the sweet taste of victory but it was far too brief.

The return flight left Dublin at ten past two and it was due to land at Llandow at three minutes past three on Sunday afternoon (12th March). There were dozens of relatives and friends awaiting its arrival. Just before three o'clock the plane was sighted about 2 miles from the runway making its landing approach. It was at a height of about 500 ft and everything appeared normal, with the undercarriage and flaps down, however some thought that it was flying a little low. The aircraft continued its shallow landing glide and one eye-witness remembered thinking at the time that if it followed that line of descent it would land short of the runway. When it was within ½ mile of the runway at a height of some 130 ft, there was a slight but noticeable increase in the noise from the engines, which appeared to reduce the rate of descent and flatten the angle of approach. But almost immediately there followed a huge roar of the engines. The nose of the aircraft started to rise slowly at first but then it went into a steep and rapid climb and gained a height of some 300 ft. Suddenly all engine noise ceased and the aircraft dropped away to starboard with its wing at an angle of 45°. It nosedived and ploughed into a field, and lay spread-eagled on its back. The fuselage was broken in two but there was no fire. As one eye-witness recalled, 'There was an absolute and deathly silence.'

The first to arrive at the scene of the accident were two brothers from the nearby village of Sigginston, who had watched the aircraft nosedive into the field narrowly missing their house. Just as they reached the

A 1950 postcard of the Avro Tudor 1, similar to the Tudor V which crashed in the fateful charter flight. After a series of inexplicable accidents, there was a question mark over the safety of the design.

wrecked plane two men staggered out with a third just behind them. They said that one of the men shouted 'For God's sake get help!' In less than three-quarters of an hour rescue appliances arrived from RAF St Athan to aid the local rescue crews and ambulances were rushed from all over South Wales. The three survivors were taken to hospital at St Athan and another ten passengers were taken out of the aircraft alive but unfortunately all died shortly afterwards. Lord Pakenham, Minister of Civil Aviation, arrived in Cardiff at 9 pm and left immediately for the scene of the crash. By midnight 73 of the victims had been identified.

It was not until Monday morning that the full scale of the disaster hit the country. In Llantarnam, a small village a few miles from Newport, five men were lost including the popular host of the local public house. One local inhabitatnt said that 'At one blow we have lost more than at any time including the war.' The newspapers called it the 'Village of Grief'. Llanharan, another small community in the valleys, was called 'The Silent Village' – there six men did not return. Abercarn, a small Gwent valley town, lost the captain, coach and star three-quarter of its rugby team. One woman from Pontypridd lost her husband and her brother. A Newbridge widow lost three sons. A husband and wife from Treforest in the Glamorgan valleys died leaving two sons and two daughters orphaned. Communities throughout South Wales mourned the loss of fathers, sons and daughters. Most of the victims came from mining areas inured to disaster below ground but this tragedy was more dreadful because of the circumstances. It had 'turned what was to be a paeon of praise into a dirge'. The *Western Mail* said 'The Triple Crown became the Triple Cross'. The newspaper organised a disaster fund and such was the wave of sympathy and sorrow throughout Wales that soon over £40,000 was collected.

The only three survivors of the crash were all sitting in adjacent seats at the tail of the aircraft. Handel Rogers and his brother-in-law, David Anthony, had only slight injuries, whilst the remaining survivor Melville Thomas was in a grave condition. Mr Rogers later said that the terrible disaster 'gave me an urge never to waste a minute of my life'. He later became the President of the Welsh Rubgy Union and returned to Ireland in 1976 to see Wales win the Triple Crown again.

The enquiry into the accident took place in the Law Courts, Cardiff in the following May and it sat for eight days. Many of the rumours that had spread about the accident were cleared once and for all. It was established that there had been no singing and dancing in the aisles when the plane came into land, that all the passengers were seated, and it was said that they were happy but tired. The number of passengers was well within the capacity of the aircraft, despite rumours to the contrary and experts considered that the length of the runway (1,600 ft) was certainly adequate for an aircraft the size of the Tudor V. It would appear that Captain Parsons on receiving the Met forecast that there was only a slight surface wind (10-15 knots) at Llandow, had expressed his view to another pilot at Dublin that 'he wished that there was a little more wind at Llandow'. However, expert opinion was given that the wind conditions were quite adequate and had no bearing on the accident. The investigators discovered that the ignition had been switched off, which could have accounted for the abrupt cessation of the engine noise before the crash. The enquiry arrived at no positive cause of the accident but it was felt that the most probable cause was the loading conditions of the aircraft, which had given a centre of gravity position considerably aft of that authorised in the relevant certificate of airworthiness. This would have resulted in insufficient elevator control remaining when full engine power was applied at a speed which, though well above the stalling speed of the aircraft, was sufficiently low to create 'a condition of acute instability'. It was further pointed out that as the luggage was not weighed at Llandow and as extra baggage had been taken on at Dublin, the load distribution was uncertain. All Tudor V aircraft were grounded after the disaster.

A fortnight later, on Saturday 25th March, over 53,000 people were at Cardiff Arms Park for the final championship game of the season against France. Before the match started the large crowd stood in silence as buglers played the Last Post in memory of the 80 victims. As one reporter commented, 'The ground was sombre with sadness, the deep emotions of the crowd were almost tangible. Victory had come to Wales at a great and almost unbearable cost'. Wales won the game 21 points to nil but the celebrations for such a triumphant season were very subdued because of that dreadful Sunday when Star Girl fell out of the sky.

The Swansea Blitz

★

It was in the darkest days of the Second World War that Swansea – 'the ugly lovely town' so beloved by Dylan Thomas – was destroyed almost beyond recognition. Old Swansea disappeared overnight leaving the town centre flattened and annihilated. As one old lady-shopkeeper said, '. . . for me Swansea is dead.'

For three consecutive nights, 19th, 20th and 21st February 1941, the town suffered such a fearful blitz that the courage and morale of its people were severely tested. It was not the first time that Swansea had been bombed nor indeed would it be the last but the ferocity of the three nights' bombing surpassed anything yet experienced by any other provincial town. Coventry had suffered grievously in the previous November as had Southampton, Portsmouth, Plymouth and Bristol but it was the first time that any city or town, other than London, had undergone three successive nights of bombing. The effect on the compact town centre with its myriad of narrow streets nestling snugly between the slopes of Town Hill and the sea was nothing short of utter devastation.

Fortunately, during 1939, the Borough Council had taken certain sensible precautions. It had always been considered that Swansea was a likely target with its busy docks, the factories of the Lower Swansea valley and the oil refinery at Llandarcy, so an efficient and sophisticated ARP (Air Raid Precautions) department was established and the fire brigade and emergency

Swansea, 'the ugly lovely town' in the 1920s, as it was before the onslaught of three consecutive nights of bombing in the Second World War.

services were greatly strengthened. Some public air raid shelters had been erected in the town centre and thousands of domestic shelters distributed throughout the town. The centre of all the emergency services was set up in the Guildhall, well to the west of the town centre, which fortunately escaped the worst of the bombing and thus stayed operational throughout the three nights of mayhem. All the emergency services had gained experience under fire as there had been raids in 1940 though mostly of a minor nature. However, there was one heavy raid on 17th January 1941, which mainly concentrated on the dock area and the loss of life was relatively light. This was said to be due in no small measure to the efficiency and excellence of all the emergency services, although sad to relate the wife of the Chairman of the ARP Committee was killed in this raid. During the three nights of aerial bombardment all the Civil Defence services and their organisations were to be most severely tested and stretched almost to breaking point.

The prelude to the first night's bombing became known as 'The Demon's Chorus'. The first enemy aircraft came in over the town and dropped parachute flares, many of which were of a chandelier pattern and appeared to be almost stationary in the sky. Whilst they were still hanging in mid air waves of aircraft came in dropping incendiary bombs, quickly followed by high explosives. It was said that the flares were so bright that the sticks of bombs could actually be seen falling through the night sky. It was estimated that up to 60 aircraft were involved in the first raid on the 19th. The following morning the *Western Mail* reported 'British night fighters went up to challenge a stream of raiders starting some time after dark and arriving at intervals over South Wales and attacking one coast town, which was the main objective.' Because of censorship Swansea was not named.

On Thursday 20th February a heavier raid took place. Soon after nightfall the aircraft came over in a steady stream and the ordeal of incendiaries and high explosives continued until shortly after midnight despite 'intense anti-aircraft fire' – there were three batteries in the area. The attack, as on the previous night, was concentrated on the town centre so it became fairly obvious the main intention of the raids was intimidation and the undermining of morale, 'terror bombing' as Winston Churchill called it. The BBC news the following day reported '. . . after two nights of heavy raiding . . . had not the slightest effect on the morale of the people of Swansea. In fact this is higher than ever.'

The first reactions to the bombing were those of shock, with people wandering about in a daze and some admitting that they felt 'flat and very depressed'. There was a strong feeling that the town 'was done for' and many expressed a deep sadness for what had been destroyed – such feelings had also been expressed in Coventry, Southampton and Bristol. In such a compact town as Swansea the overnight destruction of lifetime symbols of solidarity came as a special form of shock, the sudden loss of familiar streets and buildings had far more impact than greater damage over a wider area. A *Times* reporter later wrote of a visit to Swansea just days after the bombing, 'The men looked tired and bereft of hope and most of the women seemed to be on the verge of tears, their sadness and helplessness is very tangible.' For weeks upon weeks after the raids people gathered around the devastated town centre utterly bewildered at 'the wanton destruction of their town'. Even in 1947 Dylan Thomas bemoaned 'the flat white wastes where all the shops had been'.

Well before nightfall on the second day there were a considerable number of women, children and older people leaving the town with a few belongings to sleep out in tents and huts in Mumbles and the Gower, and this 'trekking', as it was officially called, increased on the third evening. The Government considered such activity as 'a symbol of lowered morale' and made a positive decision not only to ignore it but to actually maintain that it did not go on! Therefore those people who were not left homeless by the raids received no official help or support, but had to endure living without fuel, light, drinkable water, hot food and with little sleep. Trekking became the one positive and personal action people could take as a response to the collapse of their lives on an unprecedented scale. Trekking has now been recognised not as a cowardly or defeatist act – after all they did return the following morning – but rather as a basic survival instinct largely made necessary by a Government that failed to recognise or understand the basic needs of ordinary people living in such extraordinary times and under such extreme stress.

Shortly after dark on Friday 21st the air raid sirens wailed out their frightening warnings of another night of terror. A force of over 80 aircraft bombed the already battered town centre. This proved to be the heaviest

Oxford Street after the blitz. The loss of life had been great, and many people mourned the destruction of their familiar streets and shops at the heart of Swansea. (Photo: The Imperial War Museum)

raid of the three. The fires from the previous nights were still raging, acting as a giant beacon to the enemy aircraft. The glow from the massive fires was visible as far away as North Devon and Pembrokeshire, and it was said that the whole town was lit up by a crimson glow. The exhausted firemen fought heroically to contain the fires, undeterred by the bombs that fell about them. Most had been on continuous duty for three days and nights. Indeed the work of all the emergency services was magnificent and conducted under the most dangerous and difficult conditions. The raid ended shortly after midnight and it ensured that 'old Swansea was dead.'

During the three nights it was estimated that over 30,000 bombs had fallen on the town, causing 230 deaths and well over 500 injuries with almost 7,000 people made homeless. The town's shopping and commercial centre had been razed to the ground. The glass-domed market, the biggest and most famous in Wales, had been gutted and over 170 food shops had been destroyed as well. The tower and gaping walls of St Mary's church stood out in the surrounding rubble like a gaunt symbol of the destruction of war. Miraculously some of the older buildings had survived – the Castle, the Royal Institution, the Glynn Vivian Art Gallery and the Grand Theatre, but Ben Evans department store, which had catered for practically everything and had been an integral part of the town for almost 50 years, had been flattened.

There were endless tales of individual acts of bravery and lucky escapes. A messenger boy just 17 years old worked throughout two nights putting out incendiaries quite oblivious to the falling bombs. In another part of the town a baker continued delivering bread throughout the raids. One family had a very lucky escape when their air raid shelter in the garden received a direct hit but they were found safe but shocked hiding under the stairs! One of a rescue crew working in a bombed building felt a falling bomb graze his shoulder and, falling through the hole it made in the floor, he landed right on top of it but managed to get away before it broke into flames. There was the odd humourous story too, as when a tailor's dummy from a shop window was blasted well over 100 yards into the entrance of a chapel and it actually landed in an upright position virtually undamaged. Rumours circulated very quickly around the town. People did not believe the official death and casualty figures, being certain they were ten times more – perhaps because of the extent of the damage to the town. There was also a rumour that one of the public shelters was going to be bricked up with all the dead bodies inside. But perhaps the most persistent and widespread belief was that the raids were as a direct result of a speech by C.R. Attlee, the Deputy Prime Minister, who several days earlier had praised Swansea's war production. After the war German documents were discovered that proved Swansea had always been considered a Luftwaffe prime target. There was even a story rife in the rest of South Wales that in the days following the blitz the military had to be called out to quell civil disorder. These rumours proved quite groundless and it has since been accepted that a large part of the distress arising after any instances of bombing derived from the woeful lack of official information. The wartime Government seriously misjudged the nation's capacity to accept unpalatable news.

Swansea's immediate recovery was fairly rapid. The following day (22nd) the market was re-established over the bus garage, water and food was brought into the town and over 2,000 hot meals were served. By the end of the following week much of the town centre had been cleared and the bus service was improving, as was the food situation – even laverbread was on sale once again! Lavish praise was heaped on the spirit and bravery of the townspeople. When the King and Queen visited the town and met members of the rescue and other services as well as many victims of the raids, the public reaction to their visit was most enthusiastic. Then in April Winston Churchill came and he extolled 'the tremendous spirit of the people of battered Swansea'. The town suffered twelve more air raids in 1941 causing light damage and few casualties. The last heavy blitz was two years later almost to the very day and in this raid 34 persons died and over 100 were injured.

It was not until the end of the war that serious consideration was given to the redevelopment of the centre. The 30 or so Nissen-type shops, which had been erected on the bomb sites, had become part and parcel of the town. Several schemes were put forward and debated at length and with some haste. However, the first new road, the Kingsway, was opened in November 1950. It took the next 30 years for the full development to take shape. The present city centre fully justifies this long period of gestation, being a fine and attractive blend of old and new buildings, a large shopping centre, open spaces and walkways with the tastefully redeveloped maritime area close by. Back in the dark days of 1941 Jim Griffiths MP said 'And when the vandals are overthrown and peace comes back to our stricken world, we shall join its citizens in building a new, an even better Abertawe.' Most people would agree that this has been achieved but one wonders what the old lady-shopkeeper would think of the 'new' Swansea.

Of Floods and Hurricanes

★

For centuries the British have paid an inordinate amount of attention to the weather and despite the most sophisticated methods of forecasting now available, many people remain faithful to the old and familiar rhymes of weather lore, which have been handed down over the ages. Even as early as the 12th century Gerald of Wales was caused to remark, 'Interest in the weather is only forgiveable in those who have to make a journey by sea'. But perhaps the main reason for this fascination with weather-watching is the sheer unpredictability of the British climate, certainly it can never be thought dull. Over the years newspapers have fully reflected this preoccupation and extreme weather conditions have always been considered newsworthy, their detailed reporting having filled columns upon columns of space.

Even in the days before newspapers became an acceptable part of daily life, a report on extreme weather in Wales was not only thought to be of national interest but was considered economically worthwhile because the printed tract, entitled *Woefull Newes from Wales,* was 'solde in Paules Church yarde at the figure of the Grey-hound'.

The year was 1607 and the month was January. On Tuesday 20th, the waters of the Bristol Channel flooded hundreds of acres of land on both sides, but the worst affected area was the low-lying coastal marshes situated along the river Usk in Gwent – the Wentlloog and

Caldicot Levels. These lands had suffered flooding before this date and certainly since, but never on such a disastrous scale.

According to the tract, 'there happened such an overflowing of waters such a violent swelling of the seas and such forcible breaches made in the finne land in the counties following . . . Gloucester, Somerset, Monmouth and Glamorgan, the like never in the memory of man hath ever been seen or heard of.'

The catastrophe struck at 9 o'clock in the morning, which had dawned bright but cold. The first intimation of coming disaster was that 'they might see and perceive afar as it were in the element huge and mighty hilles of water tombling one after another in such sort as if the greatest mountains in the world had overwhelmed the lowe villages and marshy grounds. Sometimes it dazzled many of the spectators that they imagined it had been some fogge or miste coming with great swiftness towards them and with such a smoke as if mountains were all on fire and to the view of some it seemed as if myllions of thousands of arrows had been shot forthe all at one time . . .'

The waters encroached very speedily, 'no Greyhounde would have escaped by running before them' and within five hours no less than 26 parishes had been flooded and many hundreds of people 'quite devoured by these outrageous waters'. The loss of cattle, horses and sheep 'was uncountable', houses and cottages were completely submerged by the flood waters and in some areas only the very tips of church steeples were visible over the flood. The damage to property, crops and land was estimated to be over £100,000 – a natural disaster of some magnitude.

Besides reporting the facts in somewhat emotive language, the tract contains some human interest stories. A Mistress Van, who lived 5 miles from the sea wall was unfortunately drowned before she could escape into the upper rooms of her house. When one couple, who had sought shelter in a large tree, saw 'a certaine Tubbe of greater largenesse' float by underneath them, they jumped into it and were carried safely to higher land. The writer of the tract saw the disaster as the wrath of God bringing just punishment on the poor victims. He ended his tract with the hope 'that we may learne in time to be wise unto our own health and salvation, least that these water flouds in particular prove but fore-runners unto some fearful calamities more generall.'

The great flood of 1607 has several permanent reminders existing today. In St Bride's church on Wentlloog Level, there is an incription on a stone which records the height of the flood water – 5ft 6ins. When one considers that this was above the average height of a man in the 17th century, one has a measure of the severity of the flood. Over the other side of the river Usk there is a brass plaque in Goldcliff church commemorating the fact that 22 people were drowned and £5,000 was lost in the parish. And just a few miles to the east, in the porch of Redwick church is a hole 5 ft above the ground, which is simply inscribed 'Great Flood 1606'. The other two inscriptions are also dated 1606 and this apparent discrepancy is explained by the fact that then the legal new year did not start until March 25th.

Newspapers have always used the term 'hurricane' rather imprecisely. Technically it is of force 12, right at the top of the Beaufort Scale with winds in excess of 73 mph and the state of the sea considered 'phenomenal'. Recent history has shown what terrible damage can be wrought by a hurricane passing over land, even

The flood mark in the porch of Redwick Church, inscribed 'Great Flood 1606'. In some areas only the tops of the church steeples could be seen over these 'outrageous waters'.

though the Met Office was loth to admit that the very violent storm that struck southern England in 1987 was indeed a hurricane! However, at the start of September 1908, the Bristol Channel was struck by such a ferocious storm that it has passed into folklore as the 'Great Hurricane of 1908'.

In that year August had been particularly inclement with twice the average amount of rainfall, indeed on one day alone well over two inches or rain fell, which was half the monthly average. However, even worse weather was yet to come. Monday 31st August saw the wind quickly strengthening from the south west. The barometer was falling markedly but these signs were not particularly alarming as strong late summer storms were not uncommon in the Bristol Channel and the western approaches – the 'Fastnet Storm' of August 1979 is one more recent and particularly furious example. In 1908 it was in the late afternoon that the wind became a severe gale accompanied by torrential rain. During the night it continued to increase in ferocity and by Tuesday morning the local coastguard reported that a 'near perfect hurricane' was blowing in the Channel with winds in excess of 70 mph and some gusting to 90 mph. It was not until Wednesday morning, 2nd September that the weather eased and the wind moderated but by then it had left a trail of destruction both on land and at sea.

The whole of the South Wales coast suffered. Swansea was cut off from telephone and telegraph. At Port Talbot large cranes at the steelworks 'toppled over like ninepins'. Huge trees were uprooted, roofs were ripped off and at Porthcawl the sea was breaking over the harbour wall at a height of 50 to 60 ft. In Gwent it was considered 'the worst storm in living memory'. Vivid flashes of lightning lit up the surrounding countryside with the brightness of day, while hailstones 'the size of florins' were dashed against window panes. The main roads throughout the area were closed because of storm damage and the railway line between Cardiff and Swansea was blocked in several places by fallen trees. Crops were flattened and orchards ruined by the incessant and driving rain.

The storm brought havoc to the various outside functions that had been arranged for the two days. At Cowbridge, the Vale of Glamorgan Show marquees collapsed and the showground was turned into a quagmire. The East Glamorgan Show held at Caerphilly suffered torrential rain without a break; some of the tents were blown away, and the luncheon marquee was partially destroyed but the waitresses continued serving though some were said to be 'up to their waists in water'. An official was quoted as saying 'the storm was a thoroughly business-like affair' – such litotes! At Southerdown, on the south Glamorgan coast, the Welsh Golfing Union was holding its championship. The competitors struggled manfully around the course though most of the scores were over 100 for 18 holes. Two very stout and heavy wooden shelters were lifted bodily by the elements and deposited some 40 yards distance. There was talk in the clubhouse of issuing a medal to all those who had played 'in a hurricane'!

But it was at sea that the worst disasters occurred. One ferryboat captain maintained that the weather was the worst ever he had experienced in the Channel during the summer months. Throughout the length and breadth of the Channel the seas were described as 'exceptionally heavy with waves of 50 feet or more'. A Cardiff tugboat master was of the opinion that he had not known such a fierce storm in all his 42 years at sea. The severity of the storm kept most vessels in port, however those that happened to be caught out in the Channel suffered grievously.

Several vessels were stranded on Cardiff sands whilst trying to make the port. A small coasting vessel *Tribinza* struck the sands but the crew managed to get some sail on and with the help of a tug made it into Cardiff. The small Bristol smack *Francis* quickly sank just off Penarth Head but the crew escaped by a small boat and sheltered in the lee of a larger vessel until, after some hours, they were rescued. Even large vessels came to grief. The *Clan Buchanan* was parted from its three tugs and driven onto the sands, but after about three hours at the mercy of the storm, it was successfully refloated and limped into Cardiff rather damaged.

Early in the morning of Tuesday, the Helwick lightship, moored about 17 miles south west of Swansea, was being battered by very heavy seas and one tremendous wave struck the vessel leaving serious damage in its wake. The vessel was listing badly and in grave danger of sinking and a mayday signal was transmitted. The Tenby lifeboat responded to the call for help and within 2½ hours it reached the stricken lightship. With great difficulty the seven men were taken off and the lifeboat finally reached the safety of Swansea. The lifeboat crew had rowed in excess of 30 miles and had survived in such atrocious weather for almost seven hours – a magnificent rescue.

Not so lucky was the *Verajean*, a large three-masted

The 'Verajean', driven onto rocks at Rhoose Point in the 'near perfect' hurricane of 1908. (Photo: Glamorgan Archive Service)

vessel, which had left Cardiff on Saturday afternoon. With the help of two tugs it managed to reach Lundy but then the severity of the weather caused the tugs to seek shelter. The ship's master decided to beat back up the Channel to Barry Roads. By early Tuesday morning after a nightmare journey the vessel had managed to arrive within a few miles of the Roads. Unfortunately it was driven onto rocks at Rhoose point but all the crew escaped in the ship's boat and landed safely.

Further down the coast the *Amazon* had left Port Talbot but had only reached Mumbles point when the captain decided to anchor and ride out the storm. Early on Tuesday morning the anchors parted and the vessel was driven back up the Channel, where it was finally driven ashore at Margam sands, very close to the entrance of Port Talbot harbour. Out of a crew of 28 there were only 8 survivors.

When the storm had finally blown itself out local authorities throughout South Wales began to count the costs. Despite the large number of accidents there were no fatalities reported on land but there were hundreds of minor injuries and endless tales of lucky escapes. One local newspaper estimated that the damage in Cardiff and the surrounding area totalled in excess of £150,000, though one correspondent – aged 82 years – maintained that the storm had not been as severe as one in October 1866. Certainly the 1908 one does not compare with the 1987 hurricane but unlike that storm, which was mercifully of short duration, it raged for almost three days and not only left a trail of damage in its wake but it passed into Channel folklore.

Index